WOODWORKING IN SMALL SPACES

From Living Room to Workshop

Louis Kwok

WOODWORKING IN SMALL SPACES

From Living Room to Workshop

THE CROWOOD PRESS

CONTENTS

My current workspace is somewhere between the living room and the bedrooms.

CHAPTER 1

PLANNING YOUR SPACE

Space is always a luxury, especially when you live in an apartment. Every square foot (or metre) is counted towards your rent – or your mortgage, if you are fortunate enough to own your place. Identifying a suitable area for your woodworking needs is the first step on your journey to apartment woodworking. What is crucial is not how big the space is, but how creatively you are able to visualise and make use of the limited space that you have.

SPACE MANAGEMENT

If you are just starting out, I would suggest a spot where it is possible to put your tools away in a neat manner, where you can sweep up easily and keep the space relatively clean. Nobody likes a messy and cluttered workspace and having one will further discourage you from doing any actual woodwork.

There are some who convert their kitchen top or their dining table into their worktop when they want to do some woodwork and after they are done for the day, restore the area to what it was. There is no limit to where to start, but I strongly believe in being able to pack and clean up the area after each session of planing wood or cutting joints. I even know of someone who first used his bathroom as his first workspace!

Having a larger space is definitely great, but it means a bigger space to manage. It also tempts you to buy more equipment and to hoard more materials. Learning to grow organically has taught me to be a little more prudent in my purchases and to be creative in the tools and materials that I already have. I started with the only unoccupied space I had in my apartment a roughly 2 × 1m (6 × 3ft) area on the balcony.

Aside from managing the space in your apartment, you might want to factor in the access points to your apartment as well. If you are living in a building with an elevator, be sure to know what is the longest or widest piece of timber you can

My first workspace was on a balcony with a used kitchen island as a workbench.

carry into it. If you are living in a walk-up type of apartment, consider the angle of your stairwell. I inherited an old hand trolley from a shop that was closing down and found that it was excellent for transporting narrower boards of timber.

When designing your workspace, be ready to have some space assigned for material storage. Most people will think of the actual working area, but fail to organise a place to store materials and equipment. As woodworkers, our material can be rather bulky and potentially take up precious space. Depending on where you are venturing into the world of woodworking, you can quickly see your space being overcrowded by timber (or lumber) after trips to the timber/lumber yard or salvaging from other places. So, be sure to dedicate a space to house your material.

Ideally, we would want at least two working surfaces; one to do actual woodworking on, and one to put tools and other materials on. It can be very frustrating while working on multiple pieces with limited work surfaces and you end up putting stuff all over the floor which can very quickly become a safety issue. Keeping the floors relatively clear is good practice; loose power cables and wires can be a tripping hazard in the already limited work area. Wall-mounted shelving options such as the peg boards or the French cleat system are modular and can be adapted as you grow in your craft.

A WORD ON STORAGE

Always be creative with storage. I always look above and beneath when I need to find somewhere to store material. This is because the last thing you want is to play a game of tetris and to move things around just to get to what you need or to be able to start working. I have found that I can store long pieces of wood and large sheets of veneers lying flat on top of shelves or cabinets. You can also consider modifying existing pieces of furniture to suit your needs.

My second workspace was a converted bedroom in the apartment with wall-mounted shelves and a French cleat system to increase storage space.

LIGHTING

It is essential to see what we are doing, especially more so in woodworking because we are dealing with sharp chisels and saws. I generally work during the day because I enjoy using mainly natural light when I work. However, whenever that is not possible due to geographic locality or the location of the workspace, I do suggest having sufficient lighting in the work area. This could be in the form of overhead lights or portable clip-on lights. There are comparisons to fluorescent lighting, LEDs (light emitting diodes) and even tungsten lights. Which type is brighter, better for the eyes, or even cheaper to maintain?

I would suggest first using what you have before spending on a dedicated lighting system. When I first started, I used a table top lamp which uses screw-on bulbs. Screw-on bulbs like E14, E26 and E27 are convenient, because they are easily replaceable and offer various options to choose from.

There are a few things to consider when choosing your lights:

Bulbs Most bulbs come with a base. I like to use the screw-in types like E27s, but there are many others like the pin types, plug-ins or twist and lock types – even highly custom ones for special applications. This was my choice because I used what I already had, which was a table lamp that uses E27 bulbs. These screw-in types of bulbs come in a variety of brightnesses based on the wattages and lumens which you can purchase. Do consider LED (light emitting diode) bulbs as compared to CFL (compact fluorescent) or incandescent bulbs, as they require less energy and are longer lasting.

Colour temperature In the simplest terms, colour temperature is how warm (orange) or how cool (blue) the light is. Daylight has a colour temperature of around 5,000

These screw-in E27 light bulbs come in a variety of brightness and colour temperatures and can be easily replaced.

Examples of different colour temperature light bulbs on the same lamp. Warm lighting on the left and cool lighting on the right.

to 6,500K (Kelvin is the measure of colour temperature). Some people prefer working in a temperature similar to daylight because it is easier to see colours and tones. This is important when the colour of an object is critical, like when working with paints or dyes or various types of polishes.

I tend to prefer to work in a slightly warm tone lighting environment because I feel that it is more comfortable to my eyes. The colour temperature of a workshop is highly subjective because depending on what you are working on, the requirements vary. Because of this, I outgrew my table top lamp after a few years and when I was setting up my new studio, I decided to invest in LED lighting strips, which have the option to change their brightness and colour temperature, as well as them being remote controlled. It is a little luxurious but it fulfilled all my needs.

There are colour- and brightness-controllable LED screw-in bulbs available. These are very convenient and can easily convert your incandescent lamps into work lights without buying into a whole new system.

A WORD ON LIGHTING

When it is not possible to manoeuvre your lights to shine at hard-to-reach spots, get creative by using portable battery packs with USB-powered LED lights – some of these lights come with articulating arms so you can easily manipulate them into your desired position. I use old battery packs that may not be as powerful as newer ones but are still efficient in powering these small LED lights.

I affectionately call these portable battery pack lights my 'snails'.

DUST AND VENTILATION

I live with four cats, and their lungs are more sensitive than those of humans. So I try to be a responsible cat parent and also have their general health and wellbeing in mind.

I cannot stress how important our lungs are. It is also difficult to 'see' what we breathe in. Micro dust particles can be extremely dangerous when inhaled for long periods of time. I highly recommend having your set up somewhere with proper ventilation, like near open windows. If no windows are present or if it is not suitable to have the windows constantly open, then I would suggest getting at least an air purifier.

The good news is that when using hand tools, most of the wood particles produced when sawing or planing are larger as compared to using machines. This means it is possible to have most of the larger debris land on the floor, making it easier to sweep up. Some form of slip-resistant, covered footwear can help prevent injuries from falling tools and wood, or stepping over wood chips.

However, when doing any sanding or dealing with any finishes or chemicals that have fumes, it is important to wear the appropriate masks and eye protection. Some masks will only help filter out dust particles while others filter fumes and harmful gases. Invest in a good system with replaceable filters or have some disposable ones to hand.

I invested in a general purpose vacuum cleaner to clean up the rest of the dust. After each day or in between various intervals of the day, it is important to take note of how much dust is being produced and where it has accumulated on the surfaces around you. This is an indication of how the air flows (or does not) in your workspace, and how often you need to clean up. I have tried installing and using a one-horse power extractor in my home studio, but I found that it was unnecessary and was far too loud for my liking. I never have more than one power tool running at the same time, and I do not produce enough volume of dust to justify the extractor's footprint (and amount of sound it makes) in the studio.

POWER MANAGEMENT

Make sure there are enough power points for lights, possible hand-held power tools and for charging other items.

It is always convenient to have access to power points near the area you are going to be working in. This will be great for charging batteries for battery-powered tools or the portable lamp that you might be using whilst you work and even your mobile device. Just make sure you do not overload each socket and ensure that the electrical device is compatible with the power output of the country that you are in. I moved from a country which uses 220V to one which uses 110V and had to make sure I had the correct transformers.

The internet has made ordering equipment so easy across countries, so make sure you are purchasing one that is suitable with the power output that you have wherever you may be. There is some equipment which is dual voltage, which is usually denoted with '110V–220V' or '100V–240V'. This means that it can be used in whichever country you are in.

A WORD ON POWER

With so many options on power tools, consider getting a system that uses battery packs. Cordless technology has improved tremendously over the years and at the time of writing this book, most corded power tools already have their cordless counterparts readily available. Battery power packs are also typically designed to be interchangeable among the power tools.

Battery-operated tools are very convenient and eliminate the need for cords and extensions, which can become a tripping hazard.

Dual voltage appliances mean that they can be used in most parts of the world without fear of damaging your equipment.

Cats and other indoor pets have different tolerances from humans when it comes to dust, fumes and other airborne particles.

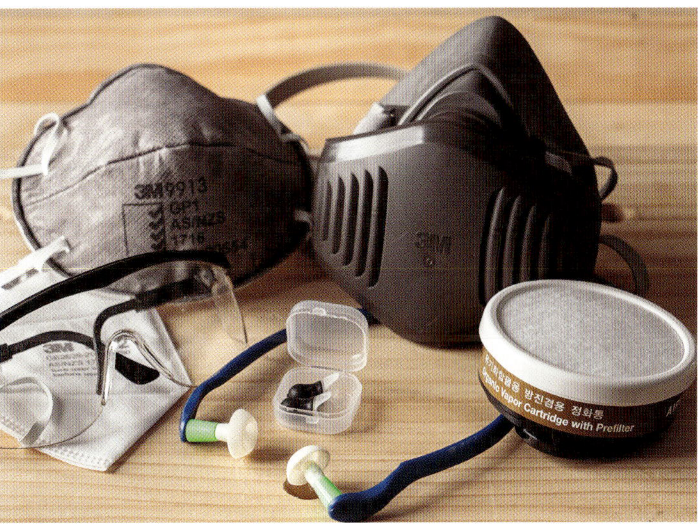

Apart from masks, eye and ear protection is essential in woodworking.

SOUND MANAGEMENT

One of the first considerations I had when I first set up my apartment workshop was how not to annoy my neighbours. The last thing you want is to have unhappy people living around you. I used to live in an apartment with three other neighbours on the floor that I was on. Thankfully none of our walls were adjacent with any of them. However, in the next apartment that I moved into, I shared an adjacent wall, so I had to take that into consideration when I was planning my workshop. The current apartment I am renting has an adjacent wall in the living room, so I have chosen the furthest room (with no adjacent neighbours) to be used as my studio.

There are two main aspects when I plan for sound.

Volume Even moving wood around will create sound. But what is an acceptable amount of sound? I take general household appliances as my guide. Using a decibel meter on my phone, I could get a rough gauge of what is generally acceptable in an apartment. Of course this varies from countries, cultures and societies and you will have to decide what is considered too loud before you start annoying someone else. The ambient sound in my area averages around 40db.

The loudest sound-emitting appliance I have is possibly my vacuum cleaner and perhaps a juice blender – their operating sound generally ranges between 70–80db.

On occasion I use a handheld router and an electric drill. Their operating sound also ranges between 70–80db. In my opinion, this puts me in an acceptable range as long as I do not use it for prolonged periods of time. I think short bursts of usage is acceptable and this also encourages you to plan your working sequence when working on a project.

For larger, fixed appliances like the vacuum cleaner (or dust extractor), you could consider making a simple sound box for it. Even a simple cardboard box with some packing foam boards will help dampen the sound quite a fair bit; you only need to make sure you leave an opening for air flow and also remember not to use it over prolonged periods to prevent overheating.

Vibrations In addition to sounds, the act of hammering, knocking or using a power tool will produce vibrations as well. I have found the use of rubber mats rather helpful in absorbing vibrations. I started laying out thin exercise mats under my workbench but found that it only helped minimally. So while setting up my second workspace, I decided to lay the entire room with a layer of 4mm natural rubber sheet as well as 18mm birch plywood. At that point in time, I wanted to make use of the sound absorption properties of the rubber mat, but also wanted the look and feel of a solid hardwood floor surface. In hindsight, it was a little overkill, but it did the job. The only problem was that, when I was moving out, the rubber mat left a stain on my beautiful terrazzo stone floor, which needed professional cleaning. If I were to apply this combination again, I would consider putting an

A simple plywood box lined with some thick foam boards can effectively reduce the sound of the vacuum cleaner by about 10–15 decibels.

underlay first before putting the rubber mat directly over the original flooring. This is especially important if your apartment is rented.

One of the best options I have used and am still currently using is thick gym mats used for weight training. These mats usually come in sheets measuring 500 × 500mm (24 × 24in) with thickness of around 2–3 inches. If people at the gym can drop their heavy barbells directly on them without causing any problems, then I am pretty sure it is good enough for the striking of my chisels!

To start off, you can choose to purchase a few pieces to put under working areas like the workbench or saw horses. You can then choose to extend the coverage to a larger area when you feel you have the need to.

Thick gym mats are great for sound absorption, as well as protecting your tools should you accidentally drop them!

For my workspace in apartment number two, I put a combination of rubber sheets and plywood over the terrazzo floor to further reduce sound.

SUMMARY: MANAGING EXPECTATIONS

Woodworking in an apartment has its limitations. I may not fit a sliding table saw through the doors of my flat, but I am still able to cut sheets of plywood using other methods such as using a hand-held plunge circular saw. There are hand tools and hand-held power tools that are able to do the same job, with a slightly different result and possibly more time to do so.

In summary, I would like to touch on the things that are possible to do, things that seem a little difficult, and things that I still have not found a solution to.

Firstly, there will always be a constant struggle with space. I have learnt much earlier that I am not able to do very large pieces like dining tables or large cabinets. But if you are a little creative with the design, you might be able to get some similar pieces done. Perhaps design them as 'knock-down' furniture, or modular systems that can transform in terms of size and shape. Because of my lack of space, I have taken some ideas found in designs from nineteenth-century campaign furniture. There are also many new types of hinges or hardware that can extend or collapse your workpiece. So, do not be limited by what you think you can do, but continue to seek solutions and this will also aid growth in your creativity.

Secondly, you might be limited by your budget. Expect to spend some money to start your woodworking journey, but do not be too eager and buy into every type and brand of tool that you think you might want. Learn to grow organically and start with a set of decent, good-quality tools. From my personal experience, cheap tools fail fast and do not do what you expect them to do. Trust me, you will end up frustrated, upset and probably feel that you wasted your money. As the saying goes, buy cheap, buy twice, or buy good, buy once.

Thirdly, it is great to be ambitious and be inspired by what you see in books, magazines and on social media. A lot of the time, the processes are overly simplified or sped up to entice viewers. Therefore, before you attempt complex joinery work, or use highly complicated and expensive products, try with simple basic joints and use organic finishes such as beeswax just to start off. Learning from the basics forms a good foundation to begin your journey. Even if you have dabbled with woodworking in the past or are already an accomplished maker, it is always good to revisit the basics; the solution to most of our most complex problems can sometimes be found there.

Lastly, try not to hurry. Rushing through a project to completion is just a quick road trip to disaster. As much as we would like to see a finished piece, it is better to have a well-made one. The act of rushing will often lead to either an accident, or a sloppy and slipshod piece of work. Have some pride in your work and make sure that the materials are used properly and respectfully. You want to make something that you will be proud of and that begins with taking time to carefully plan and execute each step properly.

There are many types of extensions, hinges, locks and other hardware that can be used in your projects.

The first few boxes that I ever made were not the prettiest, but meant the world to me.

Living and breathing, the main material for our craft is finite and should be treated with care and respect.

CHAPTER 2

KNOWING YOUR MATERIAL

For a start, we can all agree that a tree is a tall plant that has a thick stem which we call a trunk. This supports the tree and usually comes with branches sticking out with leaves on them. The material they are made from is generally referred to as 'wood'. When trees are felled for the purpose of harvesting, the meaty trunk and larger branches are called 'logs'. They will eventually be sent to the sawmill for further processing.

TREES, WOOD, LOGS, TIMBER, LUMBER

Depending on where you are in the world, some of these words have different meanings. In the United States and Canada, 'timber' and 'lumber' have their own definitions. 'Timber' is used for wood that has been cut down but has not yet been processed. 'Lumber' is used for wood that has been processed at the sawmill, possibly cut down into more manageable sizes and prepared for other purposes. In British English, the term 'timber' can be used for both processed and unprocessed wood.

Regardless, wood is the one important resource that makes us woodworkers who we are. Without this material, we are very much not 'woodworkers' anymore. Therefore, respect and consideration is important and an understanding of this finite resource should be cultivated, taking great care to ensure that it is not being exploited.

From tree to...

There are tens of thousands of species of trees in the world, but only a small percentage of them are harvested for their wood.

The process of felling a tree and turning the raw material into usable wood is a highly complex and demanding process. Thankfully, all of this work is done by trained professionals and we woodworkers have only the task of selecting milled boards, ready to be used in the comfort of our workshop. Not all trees are the same and it is good knowledge to understand their general classifications and properties.

We start by dividing trees into two categories: hardwood; deciduous trees and softwood; coniferous trees. The terms 'hardwood' and 'softwood' can be misleading because not all hardwoods are physically hard and vice versa. This classification is based on their botanical attributes. One such example is 'poplar' – a pale-coloured hardwood that is actually relatively soft and easy to use with hand tools.

Deciduous trees are angiosperms, which means that they have their seeds enclosed and covered in flowers and fruits. They have broad leaves that usually change colour and eventually drop from their branches during the colder months of winter. Deciduous trees nearer to the tropics with fewer seasonal changes lose their leaves in drier months of the year to conserve moisture.

Coniferous trees are gymnosperms which are plants with naked seeds. They are cone-bearing plants and have needle-like leaves and will usually retain foliage throughout the year.

The beauty of wood is in its range of colours, textures and even smell.

Examples of hardwoods commonly used in woodworking are: Oak, Walnut, Cherry, Ash, Maple, Birch, Rosewood, Beech and Mahogany.

Examples of softwoods commonly used in woodworking are: Pine, Cedar, Cypress and Spruce.

In general, hardwood species are slower growing and therefore are denser and stronger than softwoods, which grow faster. There are many exceptions and this shows the beauty and diversity of our fauna world.

Depending on where in the world you are, there will be wood varieties and species that are unique to your locality. I am from Singapore, a tropical island nation in south-east Asia located near the equator. Local trees include Angsana (*Pterocarpus indicus*) and Tembusu (*Fagraea fragrans*). The timber yard I frequent also has wood varieties from the rest of the region. This included Balau (*Shorea laevis*), Nyatoh (*Palaquium* spp.) and Meranti (*Shorea* spp.) to name a few. Their names often reflect the local languages and may be identified differently elsewhere. In some cases, similar-looking species are renamed and marketed by clever salesmen to make them more sellable. One such example is renaming the common rubberwood (*Hevea brasiliensis*) to 'Malaysian Oak' to make them sound more luxurious and desirable.

During my travels, I often encounter species that I have never seen before let alone worked with. One thing I learnt is not to limit your wood selection to the few commonly used ones. There is no harm in experimenting with what is available to you locally or using recycled material. Now that I am living in Taiwan, I am being introduced to species like Camphor, Taiwanese Cypress and Longan. New smells, colours and textures excite me and I am always on the lookout for interesting species that I could potentially work with.

On a slightly serious note, be mindful that illegal logging and deforestation is still an ongoing issue around the world. While it may be difficult to ascertain the true sources of our timber suppliers, we can try our best to ensure that our material comes from sustainable sources by asking the right questions and being acquainted with the ever-growing CITES list of protected species. Once again, this precious material takes years to grow and mature and we should strive to always maximise its potential and create less waste.

WHAT IS IN THE TREE?

The cross-section of a tree shows valuable information.

1) The outermost layer of the trunk is the ***bark***, a protective layer that keeps the moisture within the tree.
2) The ***cambium*** is a thin reproductive layer that continuously grows and gradually adds to the width of the tree.
3) The ***sapwood*** is the lifeline of the tree, carrying water and minerals from the roots to the other parts of the tree.
4) The ***heartwood*** is sapwood that has matured and hardened with the formation of extractives.
5) The ***growth rings*** show the age of the tree, with the space between each concentric ring representing a year of growth. Medullary rays carry and store nutrients horizontally across the tree. They are more pronounced in some species like white oak.
6) At the very centre of the tree is the ***pith***. This is the oldest part of the tree and normally not used in woodworking, as it can be very unstable and will often split apart.

Reading the rings

We have often been told that each concentric ring represents a year of growth, but what does this really mean?

During the warmer months with lots of sunlight and water, the tree grows rapidly, producing larger, thin-walled cells that allow for efficient water transport. This results in lighter-coloured rings.

In contrast, during the colder dormant months, the tree growth slows significantly or stops altogether and enters dormancy. As it heads towards the end of the growing season, the tree produces dense, smaller cells and thicker walls, resulting in a darker-coloured ring. Therefore, the combination of one lighter ring and one darker ring makes up one calendar year.

However, this might differ in trees from different geographical locations. Trees grown in temperate regions with more distinct seasonal changes have more defined annual rings as compared to trees grown in tropical regions, where the ring patterns are less apparent.

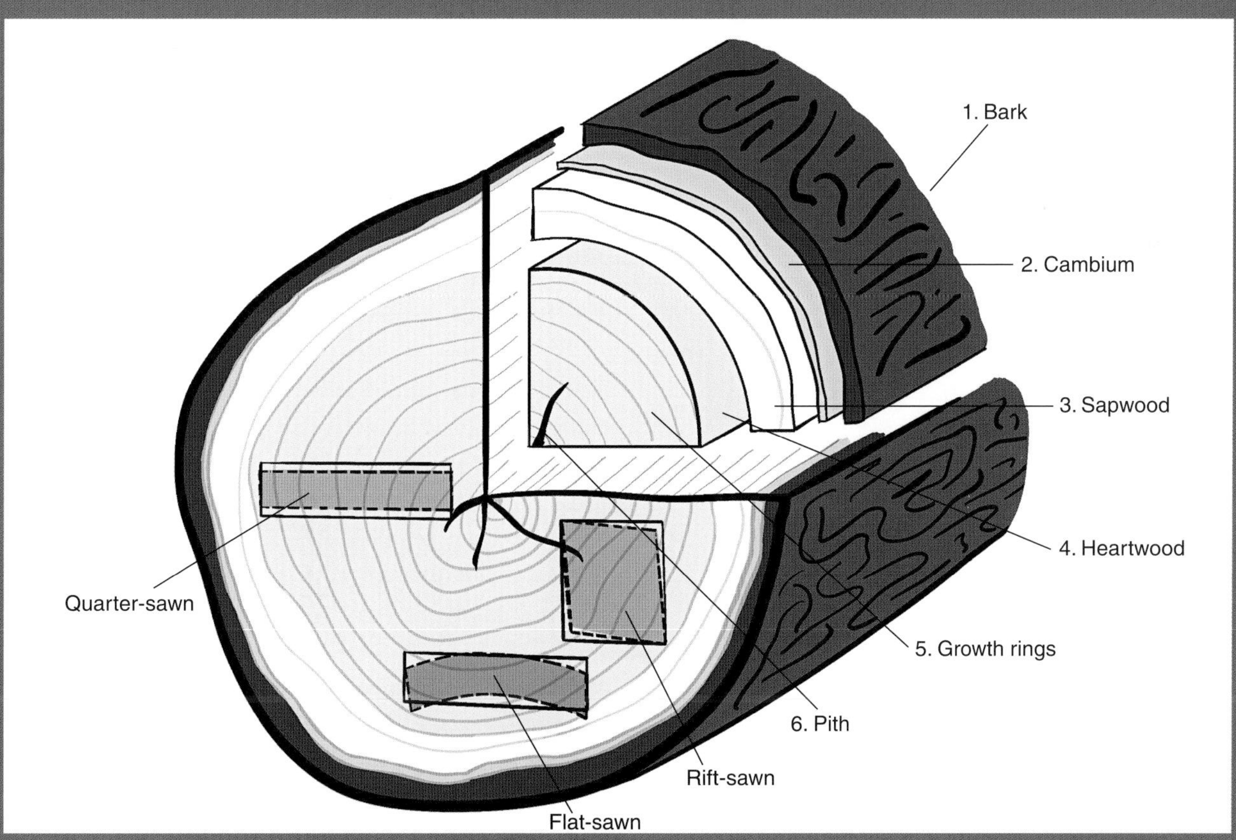

Cross-section of a tree and their main components.

CONVERTING WOOD

There are several ways in which a log is sawn into smaller boards. Even though we are normally at the mercy of how timber yards process raw wood, it is good to understand and identify the types of cuts available and how they react to the environment during our selection process.

The most common way is known as through-and-through sawing. This is the fastest and easiest way, as the log is fed through a large band saw from one side to the other in increments without any rotation at all. This method of cutting produces a range of cuts, but are mostly flat-sawn boards.

The second method is called quarter-sawing. This yields the most quarter-sawn boards and is more labour intensive, as the log needs to be rotated at various points to make the necessary cuts.

Of course there are many other ways of processing logs and it differs from sawmill to sawmill. The growth and shape of each log also determines how they should be processed to produce the best yield.

I had a rare opportunity to oversee the processing of a tree which was felled at a local construction site. It was a wonderful yet humbling experience when I took the responsibility of deciding how the logs should be milled. I stood by and watched as technicians and workers worked laboriously to move and cut the timber. By the end of a few hours, what were once four tons of large logs were milled down and stacked up in boards and rounds.

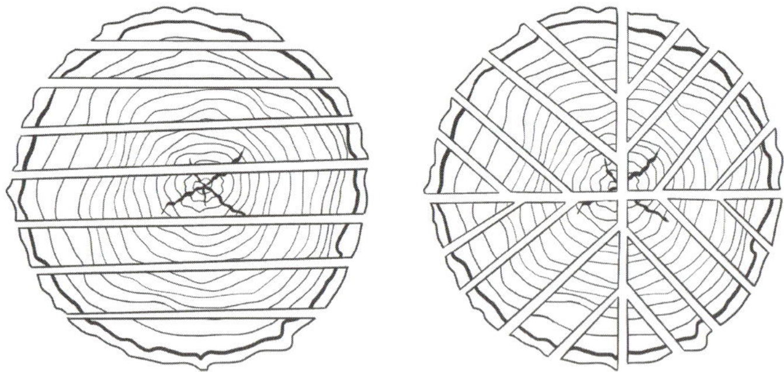

Common methods of log conversion – through-and-through (*left*) and quarter-sawing (*right*).

Large machinery is used to mill down large logs.

SOLID WOOD PROPERTIES

The different cuts of wood offer different properties and will change and react to the change in the environment's temperature and humidity (*see* box above – What is in the tree?). The three main types of cuts are:

- Flat-sawn (also known as crown-cut, plain-sawn or tangentially sawn)

The most common and widely available type of cut. The annual rings are oriented between 0–45 degrees to the wide face of the board. The surface usually has figure patterns that resemble the tops of cathedrals due to the spaces between the growth rings. Flat-sawn boards are usually not very stable and can warp and move over time.

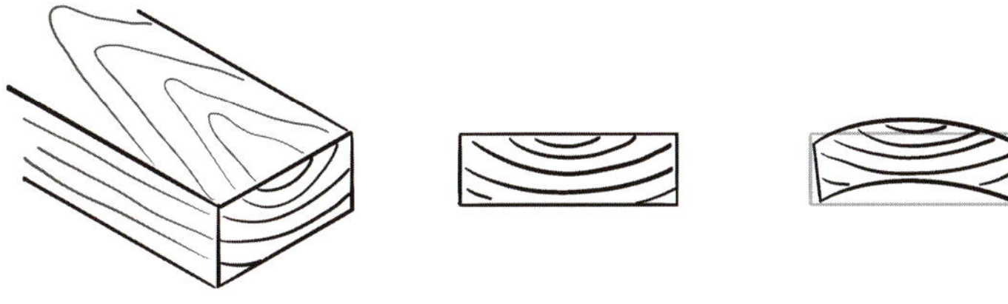

A flat-sawn piece of wood and how it might warp over time.

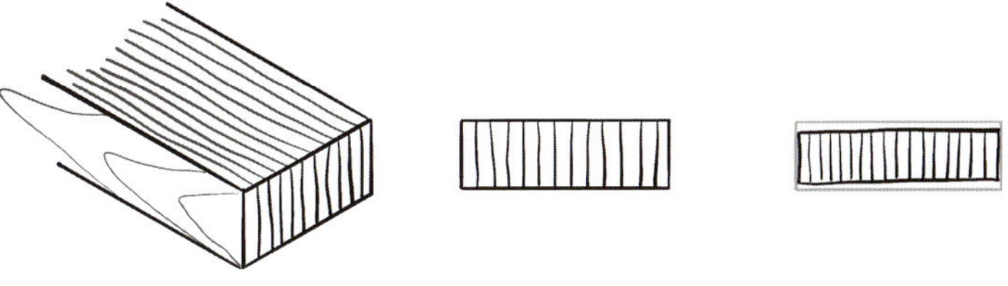

A quarter-sawn piece of wood and how it might warp over time.

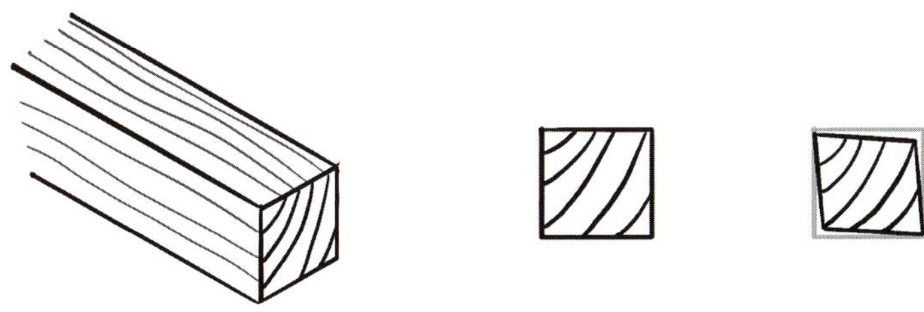

A rift-sawn piece of wood and how it might warp over time.

- Quarter-sawn (also known as quarter-cut or radially sawn)

This type of cut is identified by an almost perpendicular grain orientation to the wide face of the board. But anywhere between 60 to 90 degrees is usually considered to be quarter-sawn boards. The surface usually shows straight grains with possible ray flecks. They are dimensionally stable and are less prone to twisting and cupping.

- Rift-sawn

Rift-sawn boards are typically cut as square blanks from a somewhat in-between section where the annual rings run diagonally between 30 to 60 degrees to the wide face of the board. Rift-sawn boards tend to have uniform, straight grains on all four sides making it a popular choice for table or stool legs due to its similar appearance on all sides. They are also dimensionally quite stable.

Seasoning Wood

Once the log is converted into boards, they are stabilised through a process called seasoning to remove moisture from the wood to a certain percentage suitable for use.

This is a process whereby the moisture in the wood is reduced in a controlled and balanced manner. The two common methods are air drying and kiln drying. Air drying, as the name implies, uses the natural environment to slowly 'dry' out the wood. This is a long process that takes many years and is difficult to control due to the unpredictability of the weather. Kiln drying is much faster and can be completed in weeks. The process is much like a large oven, in which the temperature and humidity can be controlled to bring the moisture level in the wood to the desired percentage.

Even though there is a standard moisture content range in wood after the seasoning process, the range varies across countries and milling companies. Wood is a relatively hygroscopic material and its moisture levels will fluctuate based on where it is stored. In my own experience living in Singapore, where the humidity is constantly high, the moisture levels in my boards tend to be very stable. However, after moving to Taiwan and experiencing a mild seasonal change from summer to winter, I noticed that the moisture levels reflect the season. I am sure in places that experience extreme changes between seasons, the effects on the wood can be much more noticeable.

A moisture meter measures the moisture content of wood. Typical ideal moisture content ranges between 6–15 per cent depending on wood type, its drying method and intended use.

MANUFACTURED WOOD

Apart from solid, natural wood, there are many other types of engineered wood products that use a mixture of natural and synthetic material. Here are some common ones:

- ***Plywood*** is made from thin sheets of wood that are layered in alternating grain directions and bonded together to produce a uniform stable product. Examples like the Baltic birch plywood are extremely strong and stable and have a visually decorative edge.
- ***Block boards*** are strips of wood pieced together and sandwiched between two layers of plywood. They are generally lighter than plywood and used when weight is a consideration.
- ***Particle boards*** are made from wood chips and other synthetic material and bonded together with a type of binder, pressed under high heat and pressure. Generally used as a substrate for veneers or as core material for doors and wall panels.
- ***Oriented strand board (OSB)*** boards are similar to particle boards, but are made from larger wood chips and compressed with some type of binder. Some OSB boards are moisture-resistant and are suitable for humid environments.
- ***Medium Density Fibreboard (MDF)*** boards are made from wood fibres and resin, created under high heat and pressure. They have a smooth surface and are uniform-looking. Different grades of MDF also feature characteristics such as being lightweight, waterproof and even fireproof.

Among all of the above, I find myself using birch plywood the most. They come in various thicknesses and are very stable when used as a substrate. I find that cutting MDF and particle boards produces very fine dust and can be difficult to manage in an apartment. Manufactured boards are useful when larger boards are needed and when access to solid wood is limited.

When solid wood is required, finger-jointed boards are a good, affordable and sustainable option. Smaller pieces of wood are pieced together edge to edge and end grain to end grain to form a large uniform panel. They are usually made into sheets of 2440 × 1440mm (8 × 4ft) and come in various thicknesses. Because shorter sections of wood are used to form each board, they are generally more stable and produce less waste. They are also available in various wood species, from pine to oak and walnut, just to name a few.

From left: Pine Plywood, Birch Plywood, Blockboard, Particle board, Oriented Strand Board (OSB), and Medium Density Fibreboard (MDF).

Jointed boards are smaller pieces of wood that are pieced together edge to edge and end grain to end grain to form a large uniform panel.

WOOD VENEERS

This last category of processed wood is very dear to me as I am intrigued by the world of marquetry and veneers are the main material used in this form of craft.

Veneers are solid wood sliced very thinly to produce sheets (or leaves), usually used over a substrate. The thickness of each sheet of veneer can vary from 1mm to 0.6mm or even less. Historically, wood veneers were made from exotic and rarer species of wood and glued over cheaper and more abundant wood. Examples of this method of usage can be traced way back to the time of the ancient Egyptians, when wood was a scarce commodity. It was then revived in Renaissance Italian and French furniture and, in a more recent context, veneers were once again reintroduced in mid-century Scandinavian furniture.

Being an apartment woodworker, I do not have the space to keep a large stock of solid wood nor have access to machines to mill the material down each time I start on a project. I do however have some space to keep some veneers, as they are much easier to handle and store. I use veneers extensively, especially for drawer bottoms, box lids and bases, the backs of cabinets, even small tabletops and other decorative features. For me, it is always easier to laminate veneer over plywood to make up the panels that I need. Which also means that I do keep a small stock of plywood which I can cut up when needed. 4mm- or 6mm-thick (⅛ in or ¼in) plywood is more than enough if you are making items such as boxes, trays or drawers. To me, veneers are such a wonderful material, as they free up the reliance on solid wood and I can even make beautiful and interesting patterns with them which can be very difficult with solid wood.

A stack of oak veneers beside a solid piece of oak.

Wood veneers are the main material used in the decorative art of marquetry.

Left: natural veneers; top right: dyed veneers; bottom right: engineered veneers.

These days, veneers are used to maximise each log of wood. For example, from the same log of wood, rather than a few solid table tops, you can produce multiple table tops by using veneer glued over manufactured boards like plywood. This combination also produces decorative yet highly stable boards.

There are also dyed veneers and engineered veneers, whereby natural veneers are reconstituted to either form a very uniform grain figure or redesigned into other artistic patterns.

Veneers are usually sold in stacks of 24 or 32, and they are normally 8 to 10 feet in length. Their widths vary depending on the tree and also on the veneer supplier or dealer. Special veneers like burrs may come in different sizes, as this is dependent on their natural formation However, some suppliers may keep smaller-sized veneers, which may be more suitable for smaller projects.

I have ordered and bought veneers from various countries and have had no problems with shipping and customs. You may need to check on any import restrictions of your own country. Some species are prohibited in various places and this can be found in the CITES appendices.

MAN-MADE 'WOOD' VENEERS

There are several other types of sheet material used to mimic wood. One such material often confused with natural veneers is laminates, which are made of composite materials and sometimes have plastic surfaces. They are available in a wide range of colours and patterns including images of wood and may even have wood grain textures pressed onto their surfaces. Laminates are widely used because they are cheap to produce and are more durable and resistant to scratches and stains. However, they do have their own set of limitations and I find the grain patterns too homogenous and unnatural-looking for me.

Wood patterns and textures can be printed and pressed onto synthetic laminates.

SELECTING WOOD

There are many factors to consider when selecting wood for your projects. The availability, suitability, and cost. Most timber yards can resize or cut down wood into the sizes you require with an added fee; this is normally referred to as dimensioning wood.

It may be useful to check if they have any existing stock which is close to the dimensions you need. I personally enjoy going through this process because, firstly, I get to make use of material that is left over and secondly, some of this material may have been sitting around for such a long time and may be more stable and have less additional wood movement.

When purchasing wood, it is normally priced by the cost of per cubic foot or cubic metre. A cubic foot is a volumetric unit of measurement calculated as 1 foot by 1 foot by 1 foot (12 inches × 12 inches × 12 inches) = 1,728 cubic inches. In some countries, a board foot is used and this is calculated by one foot length by one foot width by one inch thick which is 12 inches × 12 inches × 1 inch = 144 cubic inches (0.0024 cubic metres).

In a simple example:

Four boards of oak each measuring 10 feet × 6 inches by 1 inch will have the volume of (120in × 6in × 1in) × 4pcs = 2,880 cubic inches. If oak has a price of 50 dollars per cubic foot, it means that the total cost of these four boards would be 2,880 ÷ 1,728 x $50 = $83.33.

There are numerous online automatic calculators and formulae available, as it can be extremely confusing, especially if there are imperial and metric conversions involved. However, knowing roughly how much a board foot of wood looks like and costs, you can give yourself an estimate of how much your project might cost you. Do factor in an additional amount of about 25–30 per cent of extra material to accommodate for test joints, mistakes and wastage. I sometimes go as high as 50 per cent, so that I have a larger selection of wood to choose from for aesthetic reasons.

SUMMARY

Unfortunately, we may not always have the luxury of being on-site at timber yards to pick and choose the best boards for ourselves and may at times end up with a mixed selection of wood quality. As wood is a natural product, we also cannot expect that every board of wood to be flawless or homogenous. Perhaps this is both the beauty and curse of wood. The earlier we learn to accept this attribute of wood, the quicker we learn to work around it or use it to our advantage.

Rather than chopping off and discarding this 'defect', on a piece of chestnut wood, it was used as a feature for this letter holder.

Hand planes, chisels and saws are core fundamental tools in woodworking.

CHAPTER 3

TOOLS AND EQUIPMENT

As you embark on your woodworking journey, one of the most debatable topics will be what tools you should be spending your money on. There is no ultimate tool list that will fit everyone, but since this is a book about setting up a home woodworking studio, the list will be geared towards that. In my opinion, there are essential tools which you will need and there are optional extras which will be great to have if you have the budget for them.

Keep in mind that tool purchasing is an investment. A well-made, good-quality tool should last a long time and keep you woodworking for years to come. That is not to say that the most expensive ones are the best, but do pause to think when looking at something that is dubiously too cheap.

The tools mentioned in this chapter are recommended based on my experience and this does not mean that there are not better options available out there. There is also a never-ending debate about the superiority of Eastern tools versus Western tools. Whichever route you choose, the most important thing is that you are able to tune up the tools, sharpen their blades and provide proper maintenance for them.

ESSENTIAL MEASURING TOOLS

Measuring and marking out accurately is quintessential to successful woodworking. With the advent of precision engineering, we now have very accurately made rulers and gauges. Tools like digital calipers also allow us to take readings quickly and we can also easily convert measurements from metric to imperial with a touch of a button.

Rulers

I use good quality steel rulers. When choosing rulers, look for ones where the measurements start accurately from the edge. This is so that internal measurements such as the insides of boxes can be taken. They are also easier to use together with other tools like squares.

I recommend getting a 150mm (6in) ruler and a 300mm (1ft) ruler to begin with. As you progress, you can gradually invest in longer rulers.

The top and middle ruler are well made and the edges are cleanly cut whilst the one at the bottom has an unclear starting edge.

A ruler stop can be very useful in making repeated markings.

Scaled drawings and models help with visualising your final project.

Some rulers have additional handy small attachments which function as stops. You can screw these attachments at fixed measurements, making them very useful when making repeated markings.

Another useful type of ruler is the scale ruler. A scale ruler is great for making scaled drawings without the need to constantly divide your measurements. It is very useful when scaling down your furniture design into a drawing that can fit your drawing paper. When possible, do look for one with smaller ratios like 1:2, 1:5, and 1:10, as compared to 1:500, 1:600 and 1:750. You can calculate mentally or omit the zero but, personally, I hate to confuse myself with all the extra digits in my head.

Drawing Equipment

I design most of my work with paper and pencil. Some pencils are great on paper but not so good when used on wood. I use an A3-size drawing board for most of my sketches and drawings. Apart from table space, I find that I can manage most of my designs in just a few pieces of A3 size paper. I do not want to have too many small bits of paper all over the place and get myself confused with multiple sheets of paper.

I would recommend a 0.5mm mechanical pencil with F or HB lead for all your layout and drawing on paper. However, I prefer to use a thicker 0.9mm mechanical pencil with 2B lead when I mark out rough cuts as they are less prone to snapping. I really hate it when the pencil lead snaps and gets stuck in the pores of the wood, they are impossible to get out and leave unsightly black streaks on light-coloured wood!

Here is a grading scale of pencils as a guide on their hardness.

4H, 3H, 2H, H, F, HB, B, 2B, 3B, 4B

Harder <——————————————>Softer

Also, good hard erasers are better than soft ones if you do use them on wood; you do not want to end up filling the pores of the wood with eraser dust.

White chalk is very useful when doing quick mark-outs on timber when visualising my project and it helps me estimate if I have the required amount of material that I need.

Marking knives

While pencils are great for laying out and marking where you would like your cuts to be, a more accurate line would be a knife line. Because a knife line cuts directly onto the workpiece creating a (hopefully) sharp depression on the wood, other tools like your chisels and blades can register against that as a guide.

A sharp and crisp line is the start of an accurate saw cut or chisel work.

From top: A double bevel knife, scalpel no. 4 handle, scalpel no. 3 handle and a custom-made knife.

Comparing the lines made with a knife, pencils and chalk on a piece of wood.

There are plenty of marking knives that you can purchase, from single bevel knives to double bevelled ones, sharp pointy ones to curved ones. There are also beautifully crafted bespoke ones with blades made from the finest steel attached to decorative handles.

Some knives require constant sharpening and maintenance. I prefer to use a scalpel with disposable blades. They can be easy to use, and sharp, and you can quickly replace the blade when it becomes dull.

However, when you think about it, the most important aspect of a marking knife is that it is sharp and makes an accurate marking on the workpiece. You can even start by using a craft knife before deciding what works best for you. Just keep in mind that when using a single-bevel knife, you would want to have the flat side against the ruler or the side that you are transferring your marking from, and not the other way round.

Squares

I have never been more confused by the variety of squares there are. Engineer's squares, try squares, machinist squares, combination squares, double squares, carpenter's squares and speed squares to name just a few!

Ultimately, the use of a square is to check for a 90-degree angle; which also means that your workpiece or wood is 'square'. Another often used angle is 45 degrees; this is commonly used for making mitre frames and boxes.

I recommend getting an engineer's square which is usually used for woodworking because it can check the external and internal measurements. It also has a groove cut inside of the 'L', allowing dirt or debris to drop through, which might otherwise affect the accuracy of the measurement.

Combination squares are also great if you just want one tool to do a range of tasks. A combination square can be used to measure both 90 and 45 degrees as well as other tasks like measuring the centre of a circle and can also be used as a depth gauge.

Personally, I use an engineer's square for most work and a Japanese mitre square when I am checking for 45-degree angles.

As with rulers, I recommend first getting a smaller square for small pieces and a medium-sized one for general woodworking.

Marking gauge

Marking gauges are used to transfer or to mark-out measurements. There are many types of marking gauges, but I find myself always going back to a Japanese-style one.

I personally find traditional English pin-types do not do a good job in marking along the grain, as the pin tends to wander where the grain goes. Perhaps it is a user problem, as I tend to be a little clumsy and prick my fingers when

Engineer squares with an internal groove help with checking for squareness.

Small squares are useful for smaller projects.

From left: English-style mortise gauge; wheel-marking gauge; Japanese-style mortise gauge; Japanese cutting gauge; notice how the gauge in my hands has a protruding nose that obstructs my view of where the blade cuts.

A Vernier calliper being used to take internal readings.

using pin-type mortise gauges. I have also tried a wheel-type marking gauge but found that I could not make exact 'point' markings.

Even among the Japanese-style marking gauges, I found one that I really liked. For me, it is important that the gauge does not hinder the view of the blade (as demonstrated in the picture above) and I can accurately see where I am pressing the tip against. I like the ones that have bent blades and can be tightened from the top of the fence with a screw, as they fit my hand well and can be used comfortably and accurately.

It is quite normal to start with one marking gauge, then gradually end up with a few of them when you have various dimensions within a single project. It is actually useful to have two or maybe even more marking gauges eventually.

Vernier caliper

I use a digital vernier caliper because I do not fancy reading off a traditional one. It is a waste of time. When measuring the thickness or width of narrower material, using a ruler can get a little fiddly if you do not get the ruler lined up perfectly with the edges of your workpieces. Another benefit of a caliper is that not only does it measure thickness, it also takes internal measurements as well as depth measurements; a rather useful tool in my opinion.

Sliding bevel gauge

A sliding bevel gauge is adjustable and can be used for setting or transferring angles to a workpiece. It can be used together with a protractor. I used them extensively when I first started cutting dovetails, but later on, I decided to get some dovetail markers, as they are inexpensive and convenient. Other uses of the sliding bevel gauge include marking-out angled legs or as a guide when drilling at an angle.

There are traditional wooden bevel gauges with a screw which I find super-annoying as I always need to have a screwdriver around, and sometimes the screw does not lock properly. I use a stainless steel one with a thumb screw so that I can lock my angle in place quickly and get on with my work without faffing around.

Other good measuring tools to have

Awl – a pointed tool to create a point on the workpiece for drilling or screwing.

Divider – A divider is useful for marking-out evenly spaced joinery or to transfer markings. They can also be used to scribe circles or make parallel lines on the workpiece.

Transferring an angle from a protractor to a sliding bevel gauge.

Dovetail markers are convenient to make multiple repeated markings.

Scriber gauge – an adjustable gauge with a flat surface like a marking gauge, except that it is used to draw lines instead of scribe marks.

ESSENTIAL WOODWORKING HAND TOOLS

Hand planes

The main use of a hand plane is to flatten the surface of the wood or reduce the amount of material by cutting or shaving it off bit by bit until the desired flatness or thickness of wood is produced. In simple terms, it is a tool with a body made of wood or metal that houses a protruding blade that does the cutting or shaving work.

There are many sizes and types of hand planes. The most commonly used ones are bench planes, which are used to flatten surfaces of wood. Specialised ones like router planes and plough planes are used to cut grooves and recesses. Spokeshaves are used to create and smoothen concave and convex curves. There are also custom-made ones such as moulding planes that have special shaped blades that can create profiles and shapes.

There are many types of hand planes, each with their own purpose.

Bench planes are referred to as such because they are commonly found on the workbench and are classified based on their size. In reference to the Stanley plane numbering system from the 1900s, no. 1 to no. 4 are known as smoothing planes, no. 5s are Jack planes, no. 6 is a fore plane, and a no. 7 to no. 8 are jointer planes. In general for bench planes, the smaller the plane, the smaller surface area it is designed to be used on, and vice versa.

If there is a budget for only one bench plane, I highly recommend either a no. 5 or no. 5½ hand plane. This plane is also known as a jack plane, which represents the 'Jack of all trades'. The size of a jack plane can be used for a variety of applications. I personally found the no. 5½ plane to be just a little too large and heavy for my hands. For comparison, the no. 4s is too short for general planing work and the no. 6 and no. 7 are too long for smaller work.

There are also low-angle bench planes which use the blade on its bevel up position. These planes are typically used when working with highly figured or difficult grain. I own one but I rarely use it, as I find my bench planes sufficient for most of my work.

A small essential plane is a block plane. It is very useful for a range of tasks like shaping smaller parts, making chamfers, flushing ends off to name a few. A block plane uses its blade with the bevel facing up and can be set to a

Comparisons of no. 4, 4½, 5, 5½ and 7 plane sizes in their widths and lengths.

A block plane is a highly versatile tool that is also small enough to be used with one hand.

higher cutting angle to tackle difficult grain (*see* Chapter Four). A block plane can also be used with one hand and I highly recommend getting one.

A shoulder plane is one of the first 'specialised' planes I recommend as it is one tool with a variety of uses. It can clean up grooves as well as trim shoulders. The blade of the shoulder plane comes up to the mouth of the plane, thus doubling up as a small rebate plane.

Other planes worth considering are a rebate plane (UK) or rabbet plane (US) to make rebates, and a plough plane to create grooves and dados; these are especially useful for box making. A router plane is also useful to make housings and grooves in wider workpieces.

Chisels

A good chisel is determined by the blade, its handle and how balanced it feels when held in the hand. Different blades are made with different steel alloys and have varied properties. Some can be sharpened relatively easily but may not hold their edge for a long time. Others can hold their edge for a good amount of time, but may not be razor-sharp.

A shoulder plane comes in handy when trimming the shoulders of tenons.

Chisels come in many types, sizes and features.

From top left to bottom right: A rebate plane, router plane and plough plane.

From left to right (*side profile and front view*): bevel-edge bench chisels, firmer chisels, mortise chisels, Japanese chisels.

It is difficult to recommend a particular brand or type, as this is determined by budget. I have had good experience with the Narex brand of chisels, which in my opinion are good value for their quality.

Steer clear of super-cheap chisels, whose only reliable purpose is probably to open paint cans.

You can start with a set of six bevel-edged chisels (6mm, 10mm, 12mm, 16mm, 18mm, 24mm). These are common starter set sizes, though you will find that you might only end up using a few selected widths more often as you progress. You can purchase chisels of different sizes individually later on if you feel that you need them for your work. I find myself reaching out for the 6mm and 10mm ones most often.

Woodworking in an apartment also means that you want to avoid too much hammering on chisels. I often end up doing more paring or slicing work to clean up dovetails and shoulders. This makes bevel-edge chisels more advantageous than the square edges of firmer chisels or the thicker mortise chisels. For mortises, instead of traditionally chopping them, I will use a hand drill to remove as much waste as I can before cleaning them with a chisel. Even if I need to use a mallet on a chisel, it will be short bursts of taps rather than continuous long heavy blows.

Other types of chisels to consider include skew or fishtail chisels, which are useful for cleaning up the insides of lapped dovetails.

Saws

I had very unpleasant experiences using the tenon saws that were in the woodwork studio in secondary school during technical class. They were of poor quality, blunt and hard to manage.

Decades later, when I was introduced to a Japanese saw, I was blown away by its ease of use and accuracy. I much prefer the pull stroke of the Japanese saw and also the thinness of its blades. Also, most modern Japanese saws have replaceable blades, eliminating the need to learn how to sharpen them.

I use a 'Ryoba' saw for all my dimensioning work. It is dual-sided: with teeth for making crosscuts on one side, and rip cuts on the other; this makes it a very versatile saw, being able to achieve both types of cuts.

A skew chisel is helpful when cleaning deep corners such as a half lap dovetail joint.

From top to bottom: A fret saw, a Dozuki saw, a flush-cut saw, two Ryoba saws and a pair of fine-cut Dozuki saws.

Double-sided 'Ryoba' saws. The side with narrower, overlapping and more saw teeth is for crosscutting and the wider, lesser-teeth side is for rip cutting.

Fret saws are great for clearing up the waste between joints.

In addition, I also have a more accurate 'Dozuki' saw with a combination blade. A Dozuki saw is the Eastern counterpart of a tenon saw and has a steel support along the spine, making it very accurate and stable when cutting tenons.

A coping saw or fret saw is useful to remove waste when cutting joinery, especially when making dovetails. They are also useful when you need to cut curves or other shapes. One thing to take note of is the clearance of the throat, which will determine how deep you can cut into a workpiece. Do look for good quality blades to use with this saw. There are blades for general straight cuts as well as ultra-thin ones used for fine marquetry work.

A flush-cut saw is useful to trim tenons or dowels protruding from a joint.

Other hand tools

A hammer or mallet is useful to tap things in place or to use with chisels. I seldom use one because I do not like to create loud, banging sounds when working in an apartment.

A cabinet scraper or card scraper is very useful in removing small amounts of 'difficult' surface material which would otherwise be very tough to work on with a hand plane. A cabinet scraper will need to be prepared and honed by using a burnisher before use.

Rasps and files are quite useful if you are doing a lot of shaping and rounding. Do note that while some metal files can be used on wood, they tend to clog up fast due to having a tight and fine grain.

The often-overlooked cabinet scraper comes in various shapes and uses a burnisher for sharpening.

ESSENTIAL WOODWORKING POWER TOOLS

A common misconception about working in an apartment is that you are limited to only using hand tools. Power tools can simplify the making process; however, they do come with a set of problems when you do woodworking in an apartment. The key consideration is the amount of noise, vibrations and dust they produce. With some of the power tools, a vacuum cleaner or extractor needs to be used at the same time to manage the dust created. This increases the amount of sound produced each time and it is definitely something to think about when you are in an apartment with neighbours really close to you.

From left to right: Brad point drill bits, Twist drill bits, Auger drill bits, Spade drill bit. *Top right*: Countersink drill bits. *Bottom right*: Forstner drill bits.

Power Drill

I would strongly recommend a handheld power drill. Even if it is not used for woodworking, it is a very useful tool to have in a home for simple repairs and modifications. In woodworking, a power drill can obviously drill holes and quickly remove material to make mortises and other housings. Traditionally, mortises are made by 'chopping' material to make holes in the wood. This requires a lot of hammering and knocking which in turn creates a lot of noise and vibrations – something we do not want, especially in an apartment. There are portable drill guides which you can attach to your hand drills; these devices help with drilling straight and act as a portable drill press. You can opt for a hand-powered manual drill or brace too, but it will take some patience and getting used to.

There are many types of bits that can be used with the hand-held drill. The one thing you might need to take note of is that a typical hand drill has the maximum shank diameter of 10mm (⅜in). Hence, you can only use drill bits that have shanks that are up to 10mm (⅜in) thick.

It is prudent to start with a simple set of drill bits for woodworking before looking at other specialised types such as forstner bits and auger bits. If space allows, a small table top drill press can be very helpful when pre-drilling for mortises.

Router/trimmer

One of my most often-used electric tools is the router. A router is a high-speed rotary tool to make grooves, shapes and profiles, and is indispensable for box making.

Most routers come with interchangeable bases to be used for various applications. Because it emits a high screeching noise when used, I tend to use the router in short bursts to shorten the high level of noise it makes. Remember to always wear hearing protection when using a router to minimise prolonged exposure to the sound.

There is a huge variety of router bits that are easily available for purchase and they are usually in two shank sizes: ¼in and ½in, corresponding to the router size that you acquire. A router is a highly versatile tool and can be used handheld or upside down attached to a base as a router table. When using it as a router table, you may consider building a casement or box around it. This can act as a sound box as well as a dust-collection receptacle.

Plunge Saw or Track Saw

In the absence of a table saw, it can be difficult to dimension larger boards. For an apartment woodworker, it is highly improbable that you can even fit a standard 8 × 4 feet (2440 × 1220mm) plywood sheet in an elevator or through your main door. I keep a small stock of 4 × 4 feet (1220 × 1220mm) plywood and even cutting it into smaller sizes can get a little tiring, especially with thicker material.

A track saw can help cut it into more manageable sizes without the footprint of a table saw. I often clear a space and make my cuts with the workpiece elevated off the ground. If space does not permit me to do so indoors, I take the operation outside on the balcony or in the corridor of my apartment. As always, my vacuum cleaner will always be attached while making cuts on the track saw.

ESSENTIAL STUDIO EQUIPMENT

- **Clamps** are basic studio equipment that you can never have too many of. There are many types of clamps, each producing their varied amount of pressure and suited for various applications. The most common types you can invest in are F-clamps and trigger clamps. Pipe clamps are very versatile in that they can be extended when needed for longer clamping and can be broken down and kept away easily. Ratchet straps used for holding things down can also be useful for clamping mitred boxes.
- **Fastening tools** such as screwdrivers and different types of screws and inserts are good to have when making jigs and simple projects. When using countersink screws, it is good to consider having a couple of countersink bits as well. There are also combination drill bits with adjustable countersink bits that can do both at the same time.

Having a range of clamps is useful for various types of projects.

Pipe clamps are extremely versatile, as they can be extended with more pipe sections to accommodate longer objects.

Ratchet straps teamed up with support blocks to clamp boxes during the glueing process.

SUMMARY

This list of tools is put together based on my own experience and preferences working in an apartment. I use most of the tools mentioned in this chapter on a daily basis and they form my core set of tools. I hope that through my recommendations, you will avoid wasting your time and money buying countless tools, gadgets and equipment that might not suit your needs.

Start your woodworking journey in a pleasant manner and not one with frustration over unsuitable tools.

Essential measuring tools:

- Rulers (150mm (6in), 300mm (12in))
- Mechanical pencils (0.5mm, 0.9mm)
- Erasers (hard)
- Marking knife
- Engineer's square (75mm (3in), 150mm (6in))
- Marking gauge
- Vernier caliper
- Sliding bevel gauge

Optional measuring tools:

- Awl
- Scriber gauge
- Divider

Essential basic woodworking tools:

- Jack hand plane
- Block plane
- Shoulder plane
- Set of chisels (6mm (¼in), 10mm (⅜in), 12mm (½in), 16mm (⅝in), 18mm (¾in), 24mm (1in))
- Ryoba Japanese saw (double-sided)
- Coping saw or fret saw

Optional additional woodworking tools:

- Hammer or mallet
- Cabinet scraper
- Rasps and files
- Router plane
- Plough plane
- Skewed chisels
- Dozuki saws (tenon saws)
- Flush cut saw

Essential power tool:

- Hand drill with a basic selection of drill bits

Optional power tools:

- Router/trimmer with a basic selection of router bits
- Plunge saw/track saw

Studio equipment:

- Clamps, screws and other useful stuff

Starting with a well-chosen set of tools lays a solid foundation for your woodworking journey.

Sharpening is an often overlooked aspect of woodworking.

CHAPTER 4

TOOL MAINTENANCE

One of the more mundane but necessary parts of woodworking is the practice of maintaining your tools and the sharpening of your blades. Bladed tools get blunt through repeated usage, and when they become dull, they are inefficient and difficult to use. They also become dangerous, because we will naturally exert more strength and force when using them. This could result in the tool slipping and potentially hurting ourselves.

There are many tools and equipment that may need occasional maintenance, and it would be near impossible to explain all of them in detail in this book. However, the ones that need most regular care are the plane and the chisel. This chapter will focus on the blades of both these tools.

THE SHARPENING STAGES

There are many approaches and different methods for sharpening tools. There are also huge debates on which methods are more efficient, cheaper, faster or better. However, be it waterstones, oilstones, diamond stones, or lapping films, they all do the same thing – which is to aid in the sharpening of your bladed tools. Therefore, before becoming overly confused about all these methods and without being partial to any one in particular, the sharpening of blades can be generally broken down into four phases: lapping, grinding, honing and polishing.

Lapping

Lapping is the process of flattening the back of a blade. This step is often only done when setting up a new blade or to recondition a used one. This is a good starting point to begin the sharpening process.

Grinding

The grinding phase is usually done for repairing a chip, or changing the angle of the blade. A coarser stone is used, as it is more aggressive to manipulate the edge of the blade. They range from as low as 200 grit to around 1,000 grit. There are also motorised grinders with stone wheels for quicker removal of material.

Honing

The bulk of the sharpening sequence happens in this phase. The main purpose of this phase is to remove any loose metal on the surface of the blade as well as to align the blade's edge. By continuously applying pressure on the surface of the blade onto the sharpening stone, you are also slowly removing any fine scratches, thus further improving its edge. The grits used at this stage are normally between 1,000–4,000 grit.

Polishing

By this stage, the angle of the blade is set and the surface of the blade should be flat and clear of most metal debris. This part of the sequence is to further create the finest edge possible by using stones with higher grits. The abrasives or stones used for this process are usually between 4,000 to 8,000. Some woodworkers even go up to 15,000 or a ridiculous 30,000 grit on lapping films. However, the higher the grit you go to does not necessarily mean that the sharper or better your blade will be. Depending on the quality of the steel of your blade, there may be a point where over-sharpening may reduce the durability or even damage the blade.

There is no ultimate setup and it varies from individual to individual. Most methods are adaptable to a small home workshop setup. The most important aspect is to be able to keep the sharpening station compact and to easily store your sharpening equipment after each use.

I keep my sharpening stones and equipment in containers for easy storage.

SHARPENING SYSTEMS

Here is a brief introduction to the common types of sharpening systems.

- **Waterstones**There are natural as well as synthetic stones, with the former being rather rare and expensive. Waterstones come in a wide variety of grits, are softer than oil stones and can cut faster. They need to be soaked in water before use and need to be re-flattened constantly after repeated use.
- **Oil stones** These are normally made from aluminium oxide or silicon carbide and are relatively affordable. Oil is used as the lubricant and also helps with the movement of the blade during the sharpening process. The swarf or metal filings have to be constantly cleared from the pores of the stone in order for them not to be clogged up.
- **Diamond stones/plates** Diamond stones or plates, as the name implies, are metal or stone surfaces with very tiny diamonds embedded onto them. They cut relatively fast and are extremely durable without the need to flatten them at all. They are used with either water or glass-cleaning fluid as the lubricating element.
- **Lapping films** These are thin abrasive films of paper thickness that have an adhesive backing that is usually stuck down onto a flat substrate like float glass or polycarbonate. Oil and water can both be used on this system and they are relatively affordable on the get go. They can be very compact and the films can be replaced easily once they are worn.

From left: A waterstone, an oilstone, diamond plates, and a glass plate with lapping films.

Entire books are written on tool sharpening and on blade geometry. There have even been scientific papers published on the optimum and perfect angle of blade sharpening, complete with high-end microscopic images.

So without being pulled too deep into this subject, I will strive to explain and introduce a basic sharpening procedure. I have chosen waterstones as the method of sharpening for this book, as this is the method that I have adopted and works well for me. Every woodworker will eventually develop their sharpening habits and methods as they go through and experiment on their own; something which I strongly urge anyone starting out to also do.

At the end of the day it is not a matter of life and death to achieve an exact 25 degrees as a primary angle or 30 degrees as a secondary angle. It could be 24 and 32 or any other number that is around those numbers. The difference is often negligible.

SETTING UP YOUR SHARPENING AND MAINTENANCE STATION

Regardless of which method you have decided on using, as an apartment woodworker, it is wise to isolate your sharpening and maintenance in to one area or to be able to contain all your equipment in one place. This makes for easy clean-up and also keeps metal shavings or rust away from other things in your home.

I use a couple of aluminium baking trays to hold any water or oil spills. A non-slip rubber mat will help to keep the trays in place during the sharpening process. I also have a small plastic box which stores all my stones and a separate container to soak them in when I am using them. I have another box that contains my sharpening jigs, oils and brushes.

The benefits of sharpening over the sink include having a constant water flow to lubricate and clean your stones. When sharpening over the sink is not possible, I will prepare a water bottle or squeeze bottle as my water source during the sharpening process.

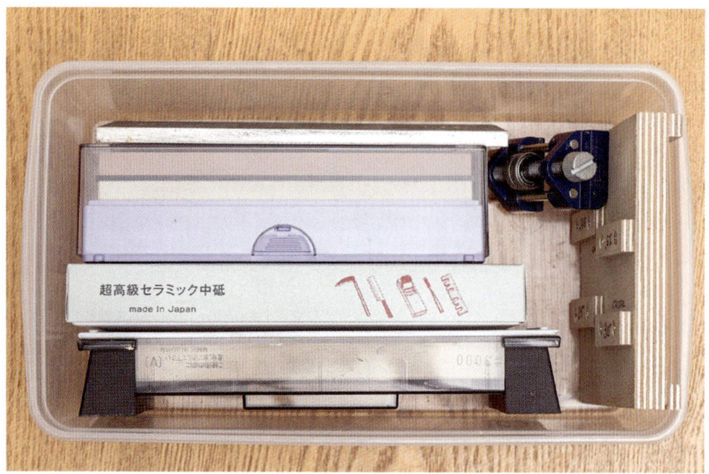

A basic set of sharpening stones and jigs.

A non-slip rubber mat can help keep the sharpening station in place.

Laying out my stones and equipment for sharpening so I can follow a sequence seamlessly.

USING WATERSTONES

I use mainly three stones and an additional fine stone for when I want to finish off at a higher grit. The rule of thumb is to gradually increase the grit as you progress. The stones I use are just a general guide – they do not have to be adhered to strictly.

1) 240/800 grit (for grinding/reshaping)
2) 1200 grit (for honing)
3) 3000 grit (for polishing)
4) 6000 grit (for final polishing)

To reduce the number of stones you need to purchase, you can also consider looking out for combination waterstones which are dual-sided. Pick suitable ones for you that cover the range of grits you need.

From right clockwise: Combination 240/800 grit stone, 1,200 grit stone, 3,000 grit stone, 6,000 grit stone, a 400/1,000 grit diamond plate and a sharpening jig.

Combination stones reduce the number of stones you need to purchase.

MAKING A WATERSTONE HOLDER

Consider making a stone holder or sink bridge that can securely hold your stones during your sharpening process.

To make a holder, you will need a piece of plywood or any other hardwood that is long enough to fit the length of your stones as well as being able to sit over the surface you will be using it on. You will also need a few smaller pieces of wood to act as stops. Measure the bottom stops to fit the area that you will be using it on if you are using it over a sink. The one I made fits the size of the trays I use, as well as over my kitchen sink.

For the top, measure the distance between the stops to fit your largest stone. You can also make two additional wedges to secure different sizes of stones. Glue up the stops using a waterproof glue like 'Titebond 3' or simply use screws, keeping in mind that most screws will eventually rust when used constantly over water.

Stone holders are useful especially when sharpening over the sink.

A pair of wedges can help secure the stones, preventing them from moving around.

PREPARING WATERSTONES

Waterstones have to be soaked in water before using. When you submerge a waterstone into water, you can almost immediately see and hear bubbles coming out as water rushes in and fills up the pores. Some stones require a longer soaking time, but a ten- to fifteen-minute soak time should normally be sufficient.

After the stones are soaked, flatten them with a diamond plate. Use a coarse side for the lower grit and a finer side for higher grit. Pencil lines can be drawn on the stone in a grid pattern to have a visual reference to ensure a well-flattened surface. Once all the pencil marks have disappeared, your stones are ready for use. To ease understanding in this guide, I will refer to these three stones as 'grinding', 'honing' and 'polishing' stones.

Soak the waterstones for approximately ten minutes.

Start by drawing a grid pattern over the stone with a pencil.

Use a diamond plate to flatten the waterstone.

Once the pencil marks disappear, the stone is flat and ready.

PREPARING A WESTERN HAND PLANE

Whether your hand plane is newly purchased or a second-hand one you acquired, it will definitely need some form of preparation before using. Modern Western hand planes generally follow a similar design, though some manufacturers might have modified adjusting mechanisms, materials and ergonomics to improve their design and performance. The processes of tuning hand planes can be very detailed and numerous. There are plenty of resources on the internet that will show you more in-depth methods of doing so. This guide will simply show you the basics of how to disassemble your plane and prepare the blade for sharpening.

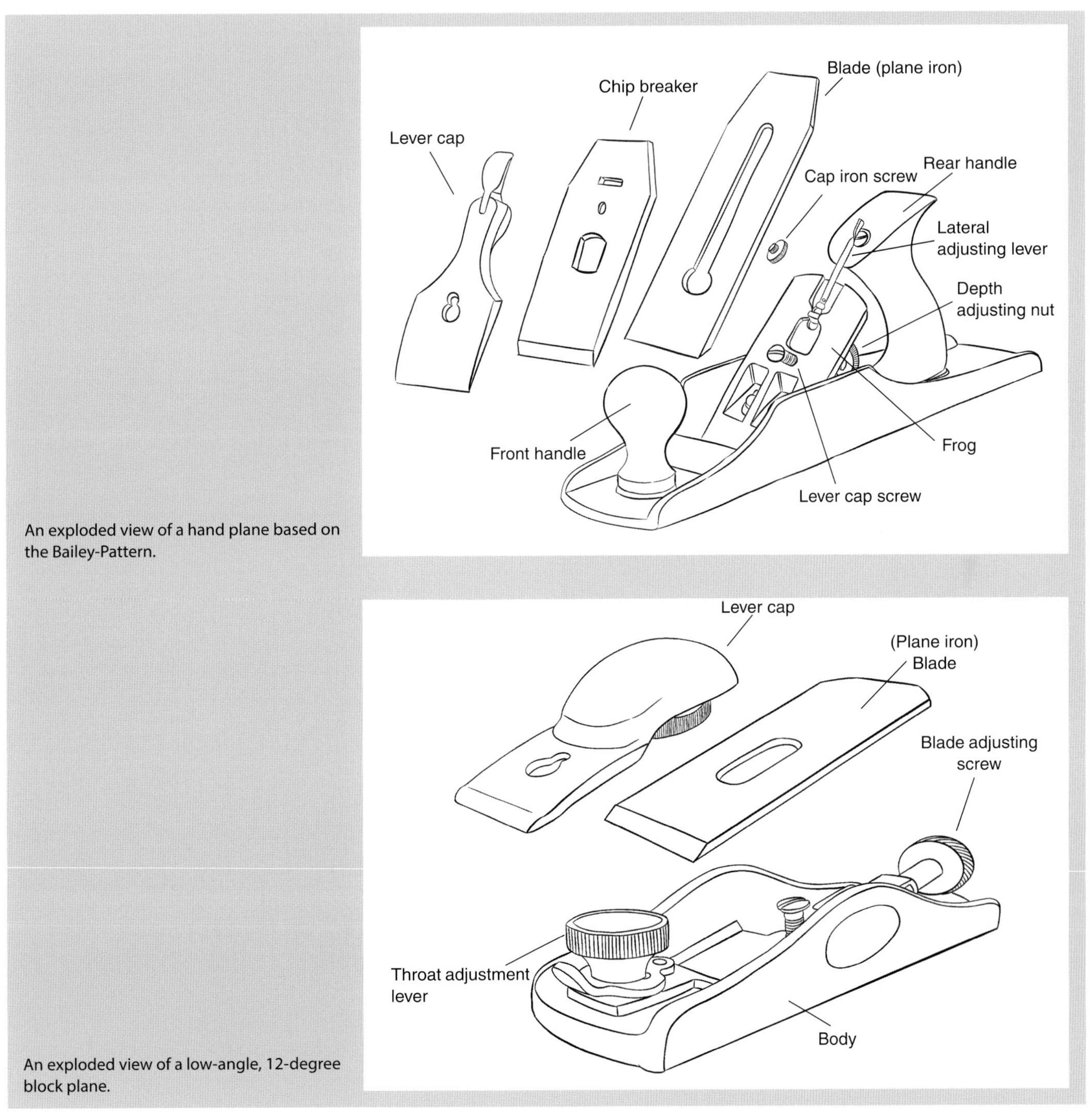

An exploded view of a hand plane based on the Bailey-Pattern.

An exploded view of a low-angle, 12-degree block plane.

DISASSEMBLY OF A WESTERN HAND PLANE

New planes normally come coated with a layer of oil. Wipe off any coatings and remove the lever cap from the body of the handplane.

Separate the chip breaker from the plane iron by removing the cap iron screw and clean the blade and chip breaker.

If dirt and rust is present on a used hand plane, remove the rust by rubbing fine steel wood or non-woven abrasive pads scuff pads with oil over the affected areas.

Clean off any accumulated dirt, especially around the knobs and screws. Brushes can be used to remove dirt particles in hard-to-reach places.

The disassembly of a typical block plane is similar with fewer parts. Loosen and remove the lever cap to unseat the blade.

THE SHARPENING PROCESS

Once you have got your hand plane cleaned up and the blades removed, it is time to start the sharpening process. This is a multi-step approach, patience and elbow grease are necessary.

LAPPING THE BACK OF THE BLADE

The first step is to flatten the back of the blade by a process called 'lapping'. New blades have 'machine marks' which should be cleared away during this stage.

The 'Ruler Trick' will expedite the lapping process quite considerably. There have been debates on the use of this method, as some deem this process as 'destroying' your flattened back and that it will take a long time to get the back of the blade perfectly flat again. On a personal note, I have tried this method on some of my plane blades with success. Try it out for yourself to see if this helps ease your sharpening process.

One very important note though; the ruler trick is not recommended for chisels, as the backs of chisels should remain absolutely flat.

1 The first step is to flatten the back of the blade by a process also known as 'lapping'. New blades have 'machine marks' which should be cleared away during this stage.

2 With the bevel of the blade facing up, move it up and down the stone. Change to higher grit stones progressively as you clear the machine marks bit by bit.

3 Alternatively, you may also use wet and dry sandpaper mounted on a flat surface with mounting spray or tape. Use some water or oil as the lubricant.

4 The machine marks will gradually disappear as the blade is slowly being flattened. A coarser grit can help speed the initial process.

5 Once completed, you can see a very distinct difference from the lapped portion and the untouched portion of the blade.

6 If you cannot polish up to the front of the blade, there is a method known as the 'ruler trick', popularised by David Charlesworth. Place a thin steel ruler under the back of the blade while lapping, which will tilt the blade slightly to produce a micro back bevel.

TROUBLE WITH FLATTENING THE BACK

If you are unsure whether you have lapped properly, especially on old tarnished blades, use a marker to draw some grid lines.

Observe how the grid lines reduce after a couple of strokes – they should slowly disappear.

Once the marker lines start to fade away, progressively change to higher grit stones and continue.

You will know you are on the right track when the front of the blade starts to get shinier and the tarnished areas disappear.

Using a Honing Guide

The most common blade angle for plane irons is a primary bevel of 25 degrees. This is the default in which most blades for hand planes come in. You can attempt to try sharpening freehand, but a honing guide can take away most of the guesswork, especially if you are just starting out. In fact many seasoned woodworkers still use honing guides, as they offer consistency and repeatability.

There are many types of honing guides, ranging from the really basic to highly complex ones with different attachments. The guide featured here is a basic one that is relatively affordable.

On one side of the honing guide, you can see some information on how to use it. Looking at the plane iron portion, you can see projection distances: 50mm (2in) = 25 degrees. This means that if you attach your blade onto the guide, the front of the blade should extend 50mm (2in) to produce a 25-degree angle. You can use a ruler to measure this distance each time you use it, or you can make a simple jig to ensure repeatability during each use.

To use the honing guide, attach the plane iron onto the holder with the bevel facing downwards. Set your blade on the honing guide to the 25-degree angle (in this case, it is a 50mm (2in) projection).

When measured and set properly, the honing guide will aid you in maintaining a constant angle during the sharpening process.

There are various types of honing guides. Some are wider to accommodate for skewed blades.

These guides have the relevant information on their sides to make your jigs.

To help with repeatability, a simple jig can be made from scraps of plywood.

The sharpening angle is set by the distance the blade protrudes from the guide.

Once set, the angle is locked in place and will remain consistent throughout the process.

SHARPENING THE PLANE BLADE

The grinding stage is where we establish the primary bevel (25 degrees). New blades may have machine marks.

With a downward pressure on the front of the blade, move the jig to and fro on the grinding stone. The bevel should be faced down against the stone.

Continue this motion until you can feel a gritty texture along the entire back edge of the bevel. This is known as the burr and is time for the next step.

Switch to the honing stone (1,200 grit). With the bevel facing up, remove the burr by moving the blade up and down flat against the stone with a consistent downward pressure.

Feel the back of the blade with your fingers to check if the burr has been successfully removed. The primary angle of 25 degrees has been established.

The secondary bevel is 30–32 degrees. Re-adjust the blade on the honing guide to the appropriate projection. Repeat step 3 but only for a few light strokes.

You will notice a secondary bevel and also a burr on the back of the blade. Repeat steps 4 and 6 on the polishing stone. The blade is now ready to be reassembled to the plane body.

THE LEATHER STROP

There is an optional step, which is stropping the blade on a piece of leather. A strop is a piece of thick leather stuck down onto a flat surface. A green honing compound, usually chromium oxide or aluminium oxide, is applied to the surface of the leather.

The blade is gently placed, bevel down, and pulled backwards a couple of strokes. This is followed by turning the blade over and lapping on the back of the blade a couple of times.

Some woodworkers argue that this step is not necessary and finishing off at the polishing stone is good enough, while others say that this improves the edge and that this can be done periodically to refresh a slightly used and dull blade. This step is really up to each individual's preference.

To make a leather strop, adhere a piece of thick leather, skin side down to a piece of plywood.

The honing compound is usually made from chromium oxide and/or aluminium oxide.

Stropping blades does not 'sharpen' them, but enhances and refines an already sharp edge.

SETTING UP A WESTERN HAND PLANE

When screwed together, the blade and chip breaker should have a tight fit with no visible light gap between them. If there are inconsistencies, remove the chip breaker and flatten the tip of the underside to achieve a flat surface.

The cap iron should be neither too tight nor too loose, but just enough to be able to make further adjustments later on. With the plane's sole facing upwards, sight from the front of the plane towards the back.

Rotating the depth adjusting nut clockwise will push the blade out of the mouth and anticlockwise will retract the blade in. Pushing the lateral adjusting lever will shift the blade left and right. The combination of both of these will help position the blade parallel with the mouth. The depth of the blade determines how thick a cut of shaving the plane will make. The more blade protruding out means a thicker cut, which also means more pressure needed and that it might sometimes not even cut through. For a start, sight just a thin hairline of blade protruding out and test it on a piece of wood. Rubbing some wax on the sole of the plane will help reduce friction when planing.

Once the blade is ready, you will need to set the blade properly back into the plane body.

Re-attach the chip breaker to the blade with a space of about 1–2mm.

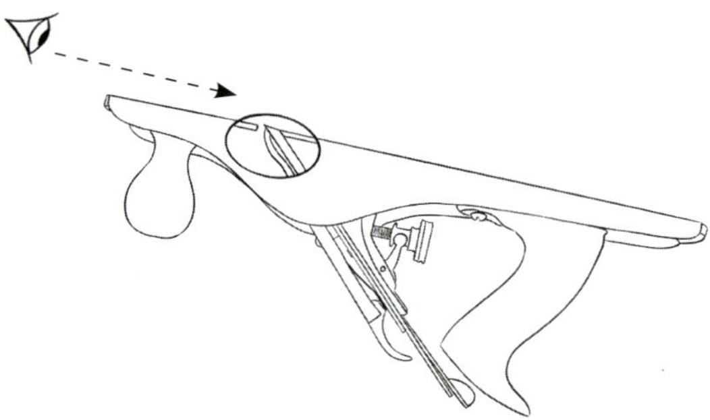

Position the plane upside down to look at the protrusion of the blade out of the mouth.

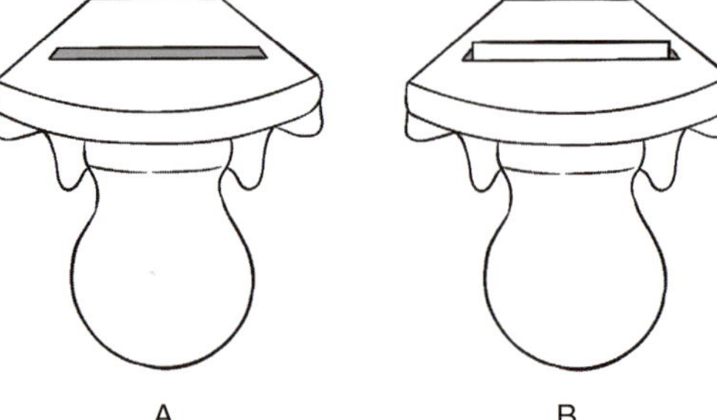

Common errors when adjusting the blade.
A: No blade protrusion – Rotate the depth adjusting nut clockwise to push the blade out.
B: Blade is skew to the left – Push the lateral adjusting lever to shift the blade.
C: Too much blade protrusion – Rotate the depth adjusting nut anti clockwise to retract the blade.

BLADE ANGLES

Most (bevel down) bench planes come with a frog set at a pre-determined angle and the blade is placed with its bevel facing downwards. A typical bench plane is normally set at a 45-degree angle, also known as a common pitch. This means that it will have a cutting angle of 45 degrees regardless of what angle you honed it to. There are other planes with higher angles, such as the 50-degree York pitch and 55-degree middle pitch, for dealing with timbers with highly figured grain.

Block planes and other bevel-up planes typically have a bed angle of 12 or 20 degrees with the blades positioned with their bevel facing upwards. This means that the effective cutting angle will be the sum of the bed angle and the honing angle of the blade.

Steeper cutting angles are normally used for highly figured timbers or timbers with grain running in different directions. The higher angle will result in a more scraping motion than a slicing motion; this will also mean that more effort is needed to push the plane across the wood.

A bevel-up plane (*bottom*) and a bevel-down plane showing their respective bedding angles.

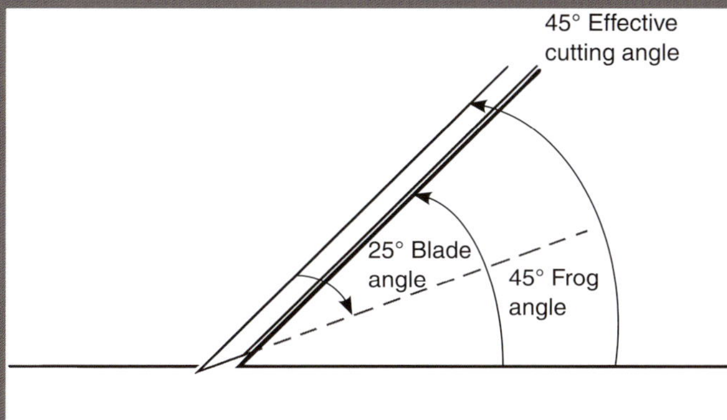

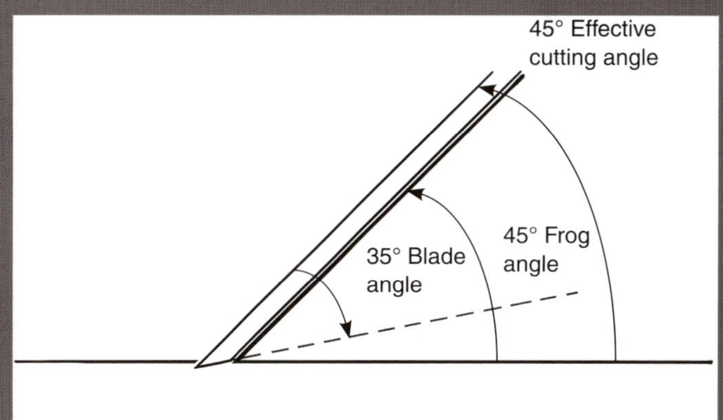

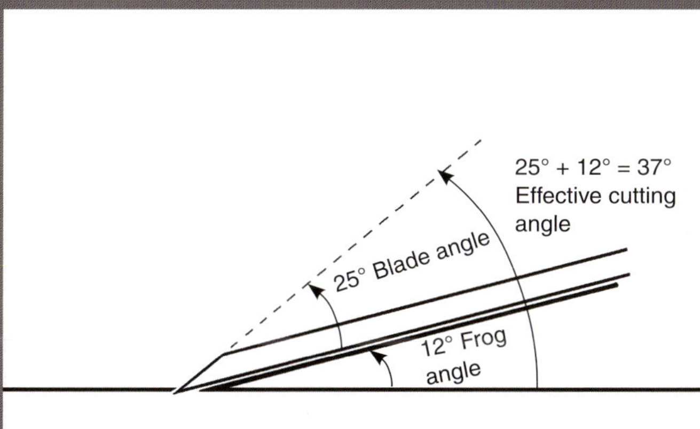

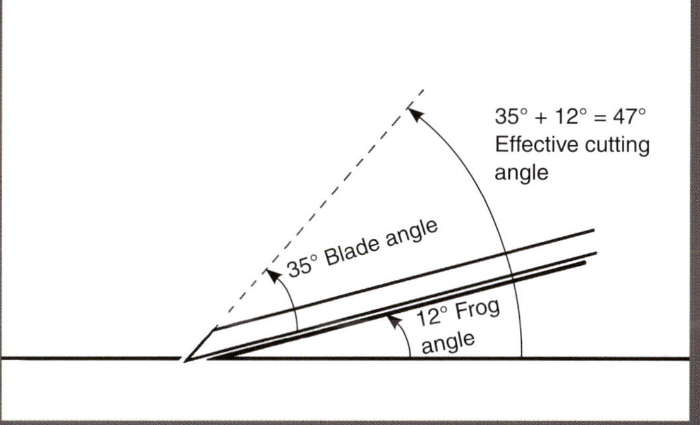

Top: A bevel-down plane with a fixed frog angle of 45 degrees; the effective cutting angle will always be 45 degrees. *Bottom*: A bevel-up plane with a fixed frog angle of 12 degrees; the effective cutting angle will change to the angle of the blade.

EASTERN HAND PLANES

Eastern hand planes encompass a variety of designs and techniques. These include the Japanese, Taiwanese and Chinese hand planes, each with its unique characteristics and technique. Among them, the Japanese style of hand plane 'Kanna' is gaining popularity and is attracting interest from many woodworkers around the world. For clarity, I will be using the Japanese hand plane to make comparisons with Western ones.

Traditional wooden-bodied Western hand planes share some similarities with Japanese hand planes. Both have a wooden body, with an angled slot to hold the blade, sometimes with or without a chip breaker. The biggest functional difference is that the Japanese planes are used in a pulling action, as opposed to the pushing action of Western planes.

The following are a few key differences between modern Western hand planes and Japanese hand planes.

- **Regular conditioning of the plane body** Changes in the temperature and humidity will affect the wooden body more so than the steel body of the western plane. For western planes, the sole of the plane should be completely flat, whereas for the Japanese plane, there are various ways to 'shape' the sole's profile for more or less contact points for different planing results.

The variety of Eastern hand planes are similar to that of their Western counterparts.

A traditional English jointer (*top*) and a Japanese hand plane.

The Japanese plane is used with a pull stroke rather than a push stroke like the Western hand plane.

The sole of the body can be shaped with a scraper to create the number of contact points needed.

- **Construction of blade** Japanese blades are made from laminated steel, are thicker and are 'hollow ground' (*urasuki*) - meaning the underside of the blade is concave so that there is only a small contact area during the back flattening process.
- **Secondary bevel and back bevel** The benefit of a secondary bevel on the western plane blade is mainly to reduce the sharpening time. However, due to the nature of how Japanese blades are forged, most of the bevel comprises of the soft steel component which is easier to sharpen, thus debunking any significant reduction in sharpening time. A back bevel on a western plane blade is a convenient way to get the back of the blade to meet the front bevel to create a sharp edge. However,

The Japanese blade is much thicker than Western plane irons and has a recessed concave underside.

The edge of the Japanese blade is made of harder steel, laminated with a softer steel on top of it.

as Japanese blades have a hollow and the actual flat part of the blade is very narrow, creating a back bevel does not make much sense and may even hinder the contact points with the chip breaker.

Some people find it a mystery setting up and using Japanese hand planes. The fact that they are so simply made as compared to the modern steel-bodied western planes makes it even more daunting when approaching Japanese hand planes. They have their own unique way of setup and tuning process and can be challenging for those more accustomed to Western planes.

Nevertheless, the most important element for any plane is the blade itself. The basic steps to sharpen the blades remain the same; a flat back and a sharp edge. Though I have to admit that there are far more steps for the actual tuning of Japanese blades.

Japanese Woodworking Tools by Toshio Odate goes into depth about this topic and is an excellent resource on Japanese tools.

I own a set of Japanese planes and chisels and do use them occasionally. I sometimes feel that the pull stroke of the Japanese plane helps my posture, especially when working on wider material. However, I do not have the tenacity to constantly recondition them. But when I do take the time to care for them properly, I find myself creating a bond and the more I understand how to tune them up efficiently. Some people enjoy this interaction with their tools and how it may influence them in their work, while others prefer less fiddling on their tools and more work time on the bench.

On this note there is no lesser or greater tool – just a matter of preference and usage. I do encourage you to try them before making any judgement.

SHARPENING CHISELS

The preparation and sharpening of chisels are not so dissimilar. They follow the same basic guidelines and principles as sharpening plane blades.

For new chisels, you may want to consider putting some oil or shellac on the handles to give some sort of protective layer on them. If you will not be using your chisels immediately, I recommend applying a thin layer of oil on the surfaces of the blade.

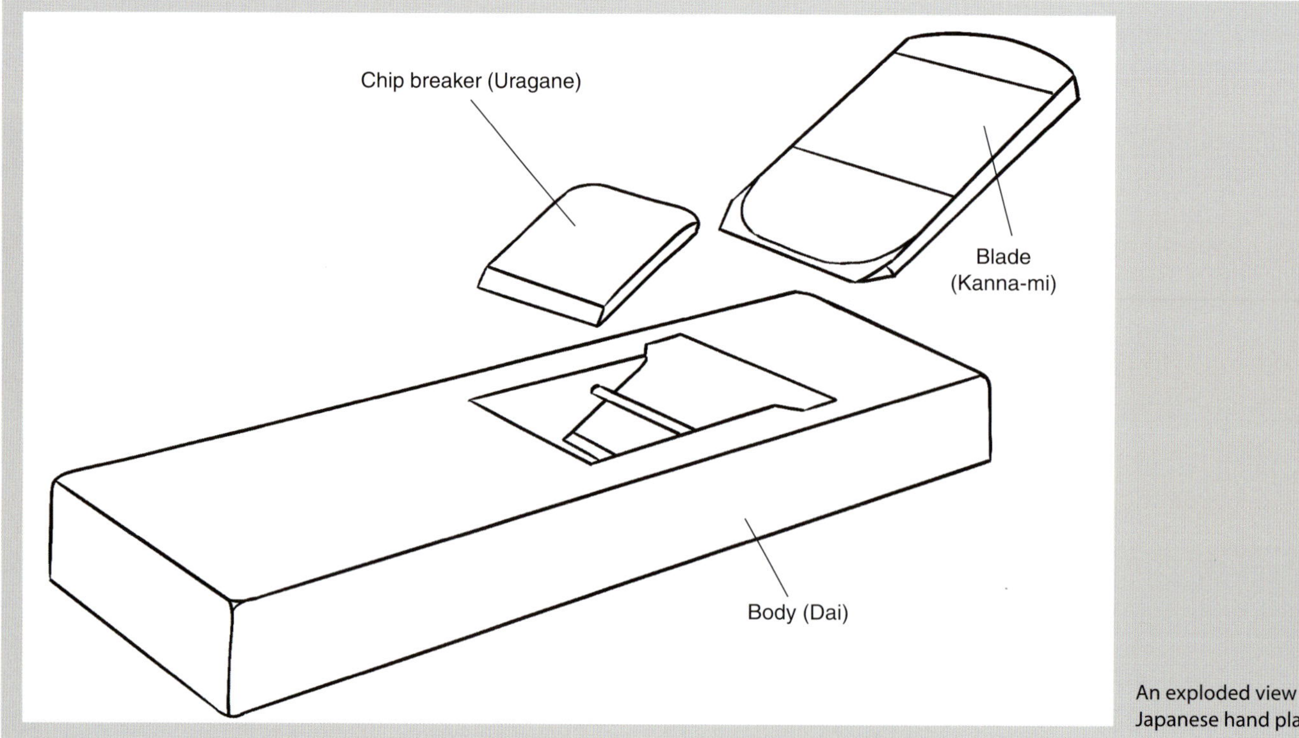

An exploded view of a Japanese hand plane.

SHARPENING CHISELS

1 As with setting up a new plane blade, new chisels may have obvious machine marks on both sides. Clean off any coatings on the blade.

2 Start the lapping process by placing the back of the chisel on the honing stone to see the condition of the blade.

3 Observe the parts which are being polished, you do not need to flatten the entire back, just the first portion of around 25mm to 40mm (approximately 1in).

4 Check the squareness of the edge. You can reset the edge with a grinding stone or metal file to establish a new squared edge.

5 Set the chisel in the honing guide for a primary bevel of 25 degrees. Start from the grinding stone and work your way until you can feel a burr on the back of the chisel.

6 Once you have established the primary bevel, re-adjust the chisel on the honing guide to create a secondary bevel.

7 Remove the burr with the polishing stone. You can also finish off by using a leather strop (*see* box – the leather strop). The chisel is now sharpened and ready for use.

A NOTE ON RUST AND CORROSION

If you are setting your tools aside, you may want to consider applying a thin layer of oil or wax to protect the steel from rust.

When iron in the steel comes into contact with the oxygen and water in the air, it will start an oxidation process which produces rust. And rust is one of the biggest enemies of woodworkers. When left unattended, the area of rust will continue to grow and affect the entire surface eventually. If you live in a high humidity location like myself, storing your tools in a dry cabinet will also help slow down the rusting process.

You can make a simple tool-oiler by rolling up some absorptive fabric material such as felt, flannelette or cotton in a tin can. Saturate the fabric with oil, then rub it onto all metal surfaces for a thin protective layer on your tools. I mainly use camellia oil, but I sometimes use mineral oil as well. I tend to avoid any oils that might go rancid quickly, and this includes most cooking oils.

You can buy a tool-oiler (*left*) or make your own with some cotton cloth stuffed in a tin can (*right*).

A thin layer of oil on your tools offers some protection to prevent rust.

SUMMARY

As you use your bladed tools, you will know when they start getting dull after repeated usage. This is the time to head back to the sharpening station. At this point, you only need to set the blades to their secondary angle and give them a couple of strokes on the honing stone. You will know when to move to the polishing stone once you feel the burr being created.

After many rounds of sharpening, you will notice that the secondary bevel will have crept up and become rather wide. At this point, you would want to consider grinding back a primary bevel and starting the process again. This process can be done quickly if you have access to a motorised sharpening system like the 'Tormek'. However, these can be very costly and might be off-putting for a beginner. I still do not own a 'Tormek' myself and have resisted getting one.

I simply use a coarse stone and some elbow grease to re-establish my primary angle when required. On some narrower chisels, I even just have my secondary bevel (30–32 degrees) as standard and do not even have a 'secondary bevel' anymore.

This basic knowledge of sharpening and maintenance will get you started on your woodworking journey. However, with each new tool that you acquire, you may need to learn how to properly prepare and care for each one of them.

From left: A brand new chisel with machine marks; a freshly sharpened chisel with a thin secondary bevel; a used chisel with a high secondary bevel; and a chisel with only a secondary bevel.

Different blades with different profiles require specific jigs to sharpen.

A simple way of holding your workpiece in the vertical position in the absence of a proper vice.

CHAPTER 5

YOUR FIRST WORK SURFACE

One of the first tasks in setting up an apartment workshop is to look for a suitable surface to start with. It should be able to accommodate the most basic methods of woodworking with hand tools, which are planing, sawing and chiselling.

Traditional Japanese craftsmen work off their floors, and it is still one of the ways of woodworking. While convenient, it may not be suitable when using Western-styled planes or doing certain chisel work.

A key element of a good work table is its stability. This is especially important if you are doing hand planing and chiselling. The last thing you would want is an unstable surface that could result in the slip of a hand and end up with some form of injury. Most tables or counter surfaces could suffice and can be modified to be used for woodworking. To help with a table rocking or moving around too much, it can be pushed against the wall or against some wooden blocks at the feet; especially towards the direction that you will be planing or sawing. Non-slip mats or rubber stoppers can also be used under the legs of the table to improve stability.

To avoid damaging your existing table top, you can use a board of wood clamped onto the table, as this creates a removable surface top that can be taken off and kept after working – much like a tablecloth, except for woodworking! A good option is some type of manufactured board like plywood or MDF roughly 12–18mm (½–¾in) thick. This gives you a relatively flat surface, which is important for hand planing. Try to find something in your home or ask around if anyone has any unwanted table tops or boards of wood you can repurpose.

The biggest gripe with not having a proper woodworking workbench is the lack of a vice to hold your workpiece down while working on it. There are numerous ways of working around in the absence of a proper vice. The simplest way is to clamp down a piece of wood onto the tabletop then clamp your workpiece to it. This can be done regardless of working vertically or horizontally. For wider or longer workpieces, you will then need a longer strip of wood to be clamped onto the table. To do hand planing, it is possible to clamp a thin strip of wood to act as a fence while planing wood.

If you do have the budget to purchase a worktop but do not have the space for an actual workbench, do consider a portable workstation. These come in the form of a small working surface with a vice and can even be used with other accessories to hold your workpieces down. They can be mounted on any existing table top with clamps and packed away when you are done for the day. A Swedish company, SJÖBERGS, makes pretty good workbenches, but there are also some other brands available on the market as well. You can also make your own, as I did with a tiny vice gifted to me a long time ago.

When I first started, I repurposed a piece of plywood I found. It was probably just over a metre long (4ft) and 50cm (20in) wide. It was placed on top of a pair of makeshift trestle legs I built hurriedly. I have since outgrown that rickety 'workbench', but it served me for quite some time. And since I primarily use Japanese-styled pull-type saws, I soon realised that I needed a lower platform to be in a more comfortable and efficient position when sawing.

I happened to have a small rectangular shelf lying around which was waiting to be installed in one of the rooms in my apartment. I used it for some sawing work and since then it has been my go-to for all my sawing needs, right up till now it never got used as a shelf.

Perhaps the point is, rather than purchase something right at the start, try and find an alternative to repurpose. This way, without spending too much, you can find out for yourself a worktop size that fits your space, suitable to the way you work. Remember you are slowly configuring the space that you have. This is a learning process and an exciting one!

Homemade (*left*) or shop-bought (*right*) portable workstations are great as worktop solutions that can be used on existing tables.

An IKEA shelf re-purposed to be used as a sawing platform.

THE BENCH HOOK

I often say in woodworking, you need to make one thing to make another. Custom-made tools or jigs can be made to help in the building of your projects. Some jigs are made for securing your workpiece in place, while others are made for repeatable actions. Complicated projects may even require multiple jigs. One of the first and easiest jigs to make is the mighty bench hook.

A bench hook is used to brace a piece of wood while it is being sawn. It is a simple shop-made jig that is made of a flat surface with two battens as stops on opposite ends of each side. The idea is that the bottom stop of the bench hook 'hooks' onto the ledge of the workbench, while the stop on the top acts as the stop that braces the workpiece.

The bench hook is normally secured on a front vice of a workbench to provide a more stable and rigid hold. This is more suited for a Western-style push saw, as the sawing motion is towards the front. However, it can still be used with a Japanese-style pull saw by using your hand to push the workpiece forward against the stop or to modify the length of the bench hook in the reverse direction with the workpiece braced towards you while you are sawing.

Traditionally, the stop is slightly shorter than the width of the base, with its ends used as a guide for the saw. This also allows the saw to cut into the excess width on the base rather than directly on to your worktop. As a personal preference, I like one of my stops to run the full width as I sometimes use my bench hook as a makeshift shooting board.

Regardless of how you prefer your stops to be, a bench hook is a versatile jig for other operations like bracing a

The mighty bench hook is the most basic work-holding jig.

A pull-style Japanese saw can also be used on a bench hook by using your hands to brace the workpiece forward.

Bench hooks are also great for spoon carving and chiselling work.

Cutting List for Bench Hook

Part	Base	Top Fence	Bottom Fence
No. of	1	1	1
Length	250mm (9¾in)	150mm (6in)	165mm (6½in)
Width	165mm (6½in)	35mm (1⅜in)	35mm (1⅜in)
Thickness	15mm (⅝in)	20mm (¾in)	20mm (¾in)
Material	Birch Plywood	Pine	Pine

workpiece for carving, drilling and even as a surface for planing smaller workpieces. Yes, a bench hook often gets sawn, chiselled and drilled into, and it is normal having multiple bench hooks as you progress.

This is a great first project, especially for a beginner, as it is simple to make and does not require perfect precision. The size of the bench hook should sit comfortably on your tabletop. You will need a base, preferably a flat manufactured board like plywood or MDF about 12mm (½in) to 18mm (¾in) thick, and two stops that are the same or slightly narrower than the width of the board. Though not critical for this project, they should still be cut relatively straight and squared. (*See* Chapter 6 on how to prepare your material.)

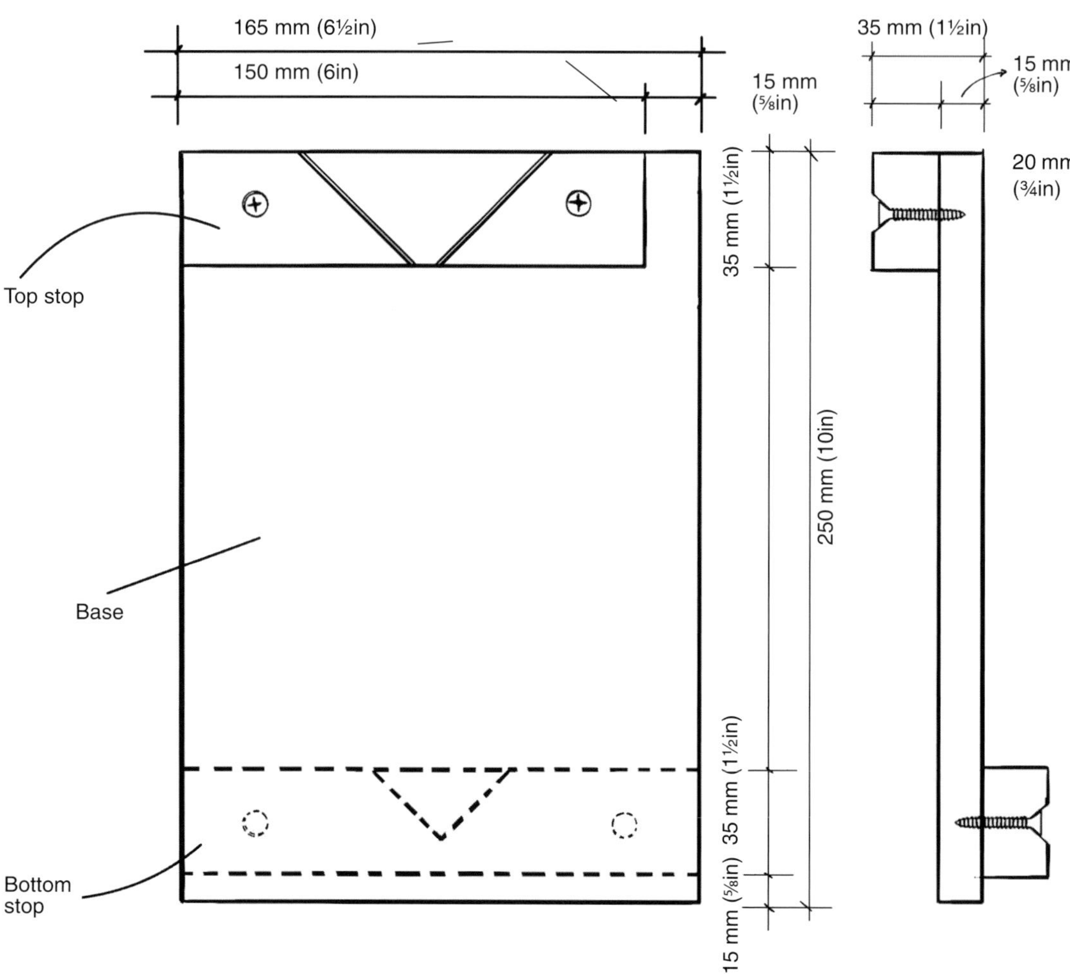

Illustration plan for making a bench hook.

MAKING A BENCH HOOK

A bench hook can also be used to make mitre cuts by cutting 45-degree kerf lines directly onto the stops to be used as a sawing guide. It is normal to cut into your bench hook, so do not worry about keeping it pristine!

The thickness of the stops can vary for different purposes. You will also need some screws and a hand drill with a countersunk bit to make some pilot holes.

Pre-drill holes for the screws and finish off with a countersunk bit or a combination bit. Put a wasteboard underneath so that you do not accidentally drill into your table top.

Position the stops directly to the edge of the base or have it offset from the edge. Clamp the stop down or secure it with some tape, making sure it is squared to the base.

Pre-drill pilot holes through the stops into the base. To ensure accuracy, masking tape can be used on the drill bit as a visual guide to mark the depth.

Secure the stops in place with screws, ensuring they are properly aligned and flushed with the base. For added strength, use wood glue between the surfaces before fastening the screws.

Repeat the same process on the other side to secure the bottom stop. Your bench hook is now completed and ready for use. I made different sizes to suit various tasks and uses.

The 45-degree kerf lines are only sawn a third down the stop and are used as a starting guide to make mitre cuts.

THE MOXON VICE

One of the most important functions of a workbench is having a vice to grip your workpiece. Even if you have a dedicated work table or workbench, installing a vice can be a daunting task, even for a seasoned woodworker. It requires accurate measurements and drilling of holes, not to mention the need for a thick and sturdy table top to install it onto. There are many types of vices which can be confusing with names like 'front vice', 'tail vice', and 'leg vice', just to name a few. While they all have their place on a traditional woodworking bench, as an apartment woodworker, it is important that you can have one vice that suits most clamping needs. Most woodworking vices are supported by two metal bars on the side with a threaded rod in the middle. This does not allow wider pieces to be clamped deep into the vice and makes working on wider boards a little difficult.

A Moxon vice is a portable and convenient vice that can be easily attached onto most existing tables with clamps and can hold onto your workpiece vertically as well as horizontally. It is named a 'Moxon' Vice after Joseph

The Moxon vice is a handy second pair of hands.

The middle screw rod of this vice obstructs the workpiece from going any deeper past the jaws.

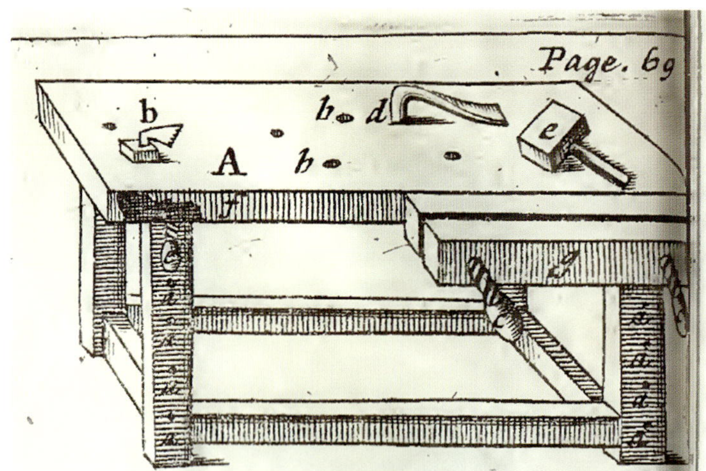

An illustration from Joseph Moxon's *Mechanick Exercises*, showing a double-screw vice on the right side of the workbench.
Moxon, J. *The Art of Joinery Mechanick Exercises: or the Doctrine of Handy-works* (Rose and Crown, 1703), p.69

There is a wide range of bolts, washers and fasteners you can choose to use for your Moxon vice.

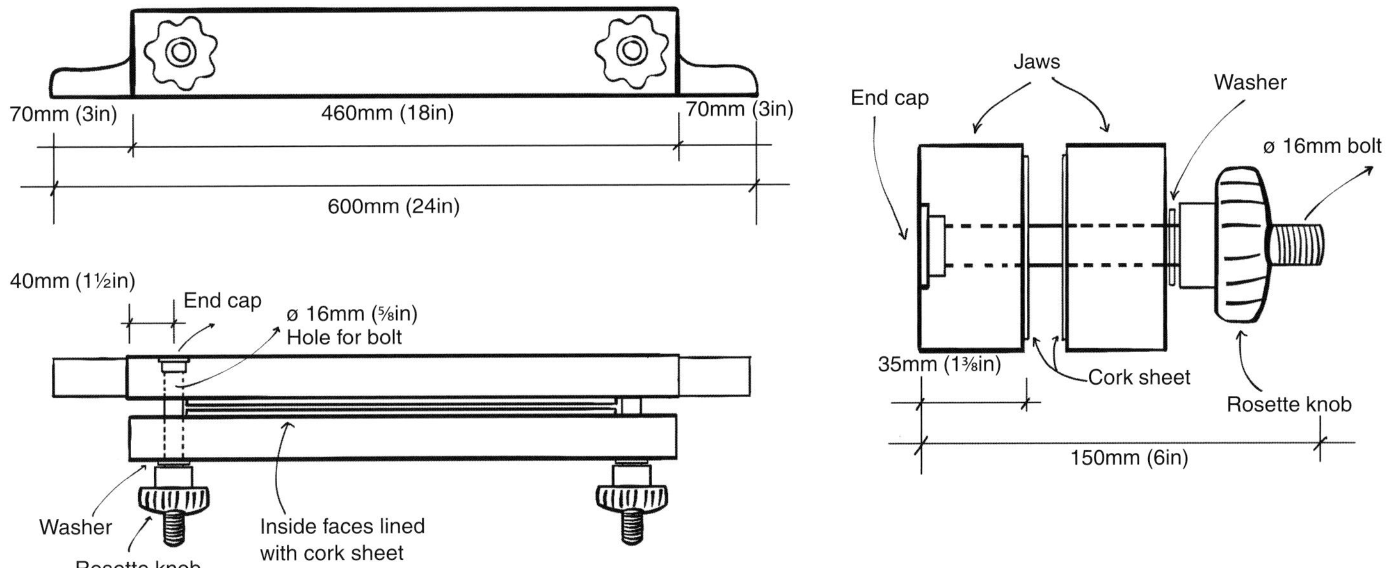

Illustration plan for the Moxon vice. The space between the jaws should accommodate most pieces.

Cutting List for Moxon Vice

Part	No. of	Length	Width	Thickness	Material
Long side	1	600mm (24in)	75mm (approximately 3in)	35mm (1⅜in)	Pine
Short side	1	460mm (18in)	75mm (approximately 3in)	35mm (1⅜in)	Pine

Moxon, who in his seventeenth-century book, *Mechanick Exercises – The Art of Joinery* described a type of double-screw vice that is attached to the side of a bench. A similar version of this type of press is also used in bookbinding and, incidentally, this was one of the first projects I made for my wife, who was venturing into the craft many years ago.

There is lots of ready-made Moxon hardware available for purchase. Some come with handles and wheels that make the movement smoother and more efficient. However, to make a simple Moxon vice, the basic hardware needed is a pair of bolts, washers and long nuts. Apart from long coupling nuts, you can also use wing nuts or other types of knobs. Take a look at your local hardware store to see what they have to offer. Keep in mind that you need to drill holes which are the diameter of the bolts, so look for the size of bolts that you have the drill bit for or can easily find.

The bolts should be long enough to accommodate the thickness of the two sides and have ample space to fit most workpieces. The ends of the bolts should have heads that are a shape that can 'lock' themselves when turned. A rounded head would not work very well for this project, while a hex-shaped or a rounded rectangle like in the accompanying image is more suitable.

You will need two pieces of wood, one slightly longer than the other so that the clamps will not be in the way when clamping on the table. I found that lengths between 300mm (1ft) to 400mm (16in) is a good range for most work. The wood should preferably be more than 25mm (1in) thick so it does not bend or warp too easily when used. I have used both hardwoods and softwoods before and have found them both to be acceptable. In this example, I am using two pieces of 35 × 75mm (1⅜in × 3in) pine and a pair of star rosette knobs with rounded rectangle bolts.

MAKING A MOXON VICE

1

The length between the bolts should be long enough to accept the widest material you intend to work on. The bolts I am using can open up to a maximum clamping capacity of 360cm (14¼in), which is sufficient for most woodworking projects.

2

On the longer piece (back piece), measure and mark the centre point for the bolts. Ensure they are not positioned too near the edge so as to have stability and strength while allowing a wide enough jaw opening.

3

Drill the holes for the bolts one by one, or clamp both pieces together to drill through them simultaneously for perfect alignment. The diameter of the hole should be exactly the same as the bolt or just slightly larger.

4

Measure the thickness of the bolt head (10mm/⅜in). Wood pieces between 4 to 6mm (¼in to ⅛in) thick can be used as an end cap to cover the bolt later on, making the total depth of recess about 15mm (⅝in).

5

Put the bolt head in position and mark the area which needs to be recessed to accommodate it. Using a marking knife to scribe the outline will help as a guide for the chiselling work later on.

6

Create a recess for the head of the bolt by starting with a smaller drill bit to remove as much waste as possible. Clean up the edges and depth with a chisel. You can tape a piece of masking tape on your chisel as a depth marker.

Ensure that the bottom of the recess is even and flat for the bolt head to sit snugly, with as little movement as possible. The remaining space above the bolt head should accommodate the end cap.

On the shorter piece, use a rounded file or wrap sandpaper around a rod to enlarge the hole horizontally. This elongated hole will reduce the likelihood of the bolt getting stuck and allow for better movement when opening and closing the vice.

An option is to cut out a clamping step on the longer piece, which enables the clamps to sit lower than the surface of the Moxon vice. You can also just use a saw to create a 90-degree step instead, providing a similar effect for clamp clearance.

By using cork sheets to line the inside faces, you can increase the grip of the vice.

Some woodworkers also use suede or sandpaper for added friction; just make sure that the material will not damage your workpiece.

Assemble the parts of the vice and shape the end caps to fit over the bolt head. You can most definitely leave the bolt head exposed, but it is recommended to glue it in place with adhesive to prevent it from being pushed out during use.

Adhere the end cap in place and saw off or plane the excess to flush the surface. Your Moxon vice is now ready for use. You can consider using a different-coloured wood for the end cap for some visual interest.

To use the Moxon vice, clamp down the longer piece of wood on the work surface with the shorter piece off the table.

The Moxon vice is ideal for clamping wider boards vertically, allowing for better control and stability.

The Moxon vice can also be used to clamp a long workpiece for edge planing, especially useful for thinner, narrower boards.

SUMMARY

Starting out in an apartment will certainly have its limitations and challenges. Do not be discouraged by the lack of space and proper woodworking equipment. I remember when my first woodworking teacher, Mr Hou, said to me that we needed a bench hook, all I could think of was to go to the local craft shop to buy one – not realising that, even as a beginner, I had the ability to put together some pieces of wood to actually make one on the spot. I am also always constantly keeping a look out for items to modify and repurpose for apartment woodworking.

My first bench hook and Moxon vice have certainly seen better days.

The hand plane, saw and chisels; three basic woodworking tools.

CHAPTER 6

WOODWORKING BASICS

The three basic hand tools for woodworking in my opinion are the saw, the hand plane and the chisel. The combination of these tools will allow you to start making projects. In this chapter we will learn how to use the saw and hand plane in conjunction with other measuring tools such as the square and the marking gauge. We will also learn how to prepare your material, which is an important start to any making process. The use of chisels will be covered in the next chapter when we will be introducing joinery.

SAWING

Whilst you can purchase ready-cut timber from timber yards to your specified dimensions, nothing beats knowing how to resaw and dimension your own material at home. Whether you use a Western-style push saw or a Japanese-style pull saw, the hand saw is an efficient cutting machine once you know how to use it properly. As mentioned in Chapter Three, there are generally two types of saws: the crosscut saw and the rip cut saw. I use a Japanese combination saw which has both sets of teeth. Crosscutting cuts across the grain of the wood while ripping cuts along the grain of the wood.

I mainly use Japanese pull-style saws, and this is done mostly on a lower work surface. I find that propping the workpiece on a low stool against a bench hook and using my body weight to hold it down is an efficient way of sawing. You can also use clamps to secure your material down for more stability.

Use the correct side of the saw for the appropriate cut; *Left*: crosscut for cutting across the grain of the wood, and; *Right*: rip cut for ripping lengthwise.

While pulling your workpiece against a bench hook, use your knuckles to guide the saw into its correct starting position.

Tilt the saw in various angles to get a feel of how each angle affects the sawing experience.

Draw a line where you intend to saw. To start the cut, hold the workpiece down and use your thumb's middle knuckle to guide the saw into the starting mark. Push the saw forwards and then gently pull it backwards. The Japanese saw operates on the pull cut, so more pressure is applied on the pull stroke. And because of this, there will be noticeably more debris at the back of the saw, thus hindering the marking line. I tend to place my saw on the right side of the pencil line so that I can continue to follow the line as I make my cut.

Continue sawing whilst following the line, perhaps trying different sawing angles by tilting the saw upwards or downwards (not sideways) to get a feel for an efficient angle. Depending on the size of the workpiece, you can also rotate it and follow the marking line as you saw. When you are nearing the end of the cut, slow down and gently finish off. To prevent the sawn wood from falling onto the ground, you can consider placing a gym mat or place a slightly lower platform like a box or a stool as a support to reduce the sound of wood knocking directly onto the floor.

GRAIN DIRECTION

Once your material is a more manageable size, we can start to prepare it by using a hand plane to flatten the surfaces. However, before we start planing, the first thing we need to identify is the grain direction of wood. Imagine brushing a cat or a dog, you will want to brush along the fur and not against it (which will make a very angry animal!). This is very much the same concept as when identifying grain direction and deciding which direction to plane from.

To plane the faces, you need to look at the grain direction on the edges. You will notice lines moving from the bottom to the top or vice versa. The direction you will want to plane in is as if you are brushing the cat; the lower end is akin to the skin and the top end is the surface of the fur. You plane in the direction where the lines are moving from bottom to top. This is normally called planing 'uphill'.

Identifying grain direction can be tricky at first, because it may not be easy to identify which lines to look at. Often, you may also encounter lines that come up from both sides and look like 'hills' or 'valleys'. Some species of timber are highly 'figured' and you may see pattern-like swirls, almost like a painting.

When approaching 'hills' and 'valleys', some woodworkers plane from or towards both sides respectively, others plane towards the direction where the majority of the surface is along the grain.

Highly figured timbers in which there is no clear direction of grain can be a challenge to plane, as tear outs will be common. When I first started out, I sometimes avoided them altogether, as tackling them properly meant that I had to bring out my low-angle plane. I have since invested in a spare plane blade for my block plane, which is sharpened to a 40-degree angle to tackle such timbers. But still I tend to be more cautious when approaching such timbers. If the highly figured surface is generally flat to begin with, a cabinet scraper can also be used for dressing the surface.

Regardless of what is seen visually, try and get a sense of what it feels like planing along the grain, and planing against the grain. You will find that planing along the grain feels smooth and agreeable, and planing against the grain has more resistance and friction as you move your plane along. In most cases, planing along the grain will result in a smooth, even surface with almost full shavings and planing against the grain will result in an uneven surface with broken shavings, and might sometimes even rip out the fibres, causing tear outs and damaging your surface.

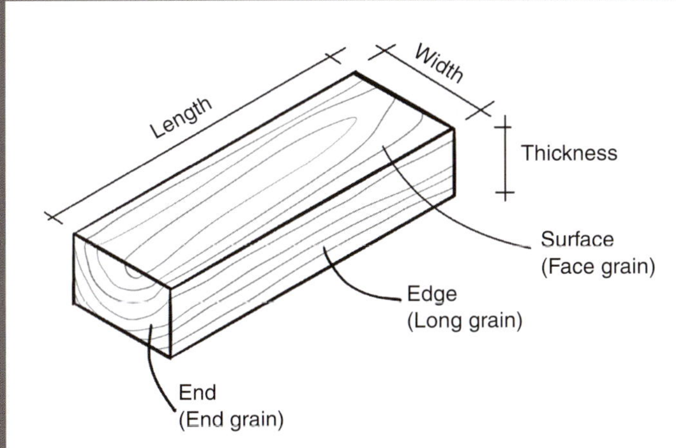

Terminology and parts of wood.

To plane the face, look at the grain information on the edge.

Wood grain differs not only from species to species but also according to how the log was milled, creating a wide range of patterns and appearances.

Top: Grain direction is generally flowing upwards from left to right. *Middle*: Grain direction is coming towards the centre like a 'hill'. *Bottom*: Grain direction is highly figured and is difficult to identify.

Two pieces of ash; the piece on the left was planed along the grain and leaves a smooth finish while the piece on the right was planed against the grain and leaves an uneven surface.

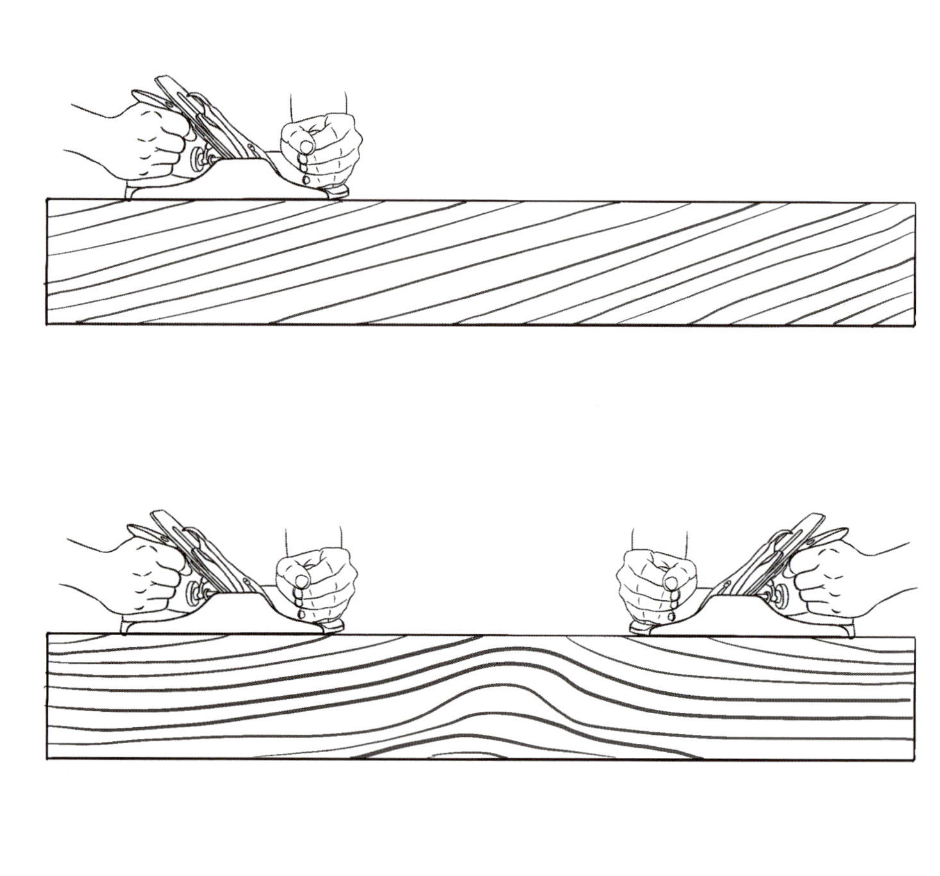

Illustration showing the direction of the plane according to the grain direction of the wood.

PLANING

The main use of a hand plane is to flatten the surface of wood. Using the hand plane efficiently is a correct combination of pressure, direction and motion.

Squaring up using a hand plane

To 'square' a piece of wood means that all four sides should be flat and are 90 degrees at all four corners. This also means 'surfaced four sides' and is normally abbreviated by 'S4S', which is common lingo at timber yards.

To begin, take a straightedge like a ruler or the blade of the square and place it on the wider surface across the face of the wood. Point it against a light source and see the profile created between the straight edge and the surface of the wood. Try to place the straight edge on various parts along the length of the wood to get an overall reading.

While we hope to see a flat surface without any bumps or unevenness, it is usually not the case. Instead, the above illustration shows (in exaggeration) a few common scenarios. Looking from the end grain of the piece of wood, the left diagram shows the surface cupped upwards, which means that you need to plane off the highlighted middle area to achieve a flat surface. The middle diagram shows the surface cupped downwards, which means that you need to plane off the highlighted sides to achieve a flat surface, as shown in the accompanying diagram on the right.

Next, use a long ruler to check the length of the wood to see if it is bowed or twisted. The more unevenness there is, the more work needs to be done to prepare the wood to make it flat and square. It does take some getting used to

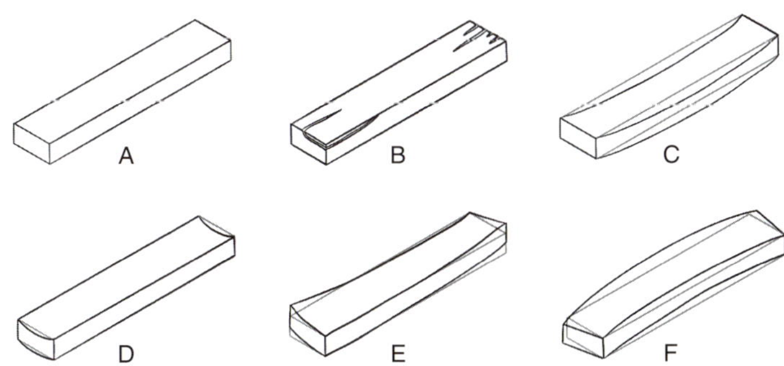

A: A piece of wood with no warping; B: crack and split; C: bow; D: cup; E: twist; F: crook.

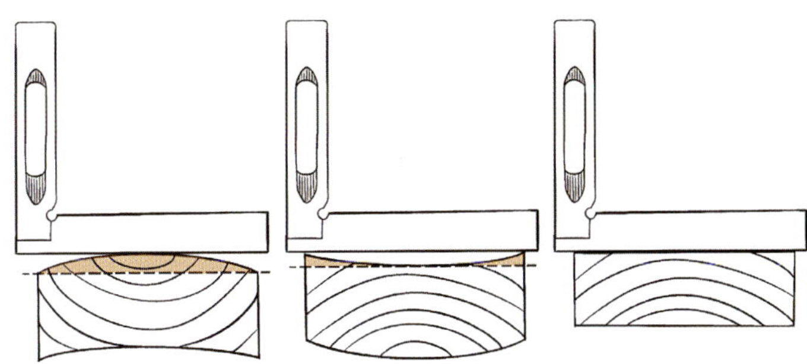

Left and middle: Cupped surfaces which need to be planed. *Right*: A flat surface, which is ideal.

When holding the hand plane, grip both handles firmly and use your legs to stabilise your stance.

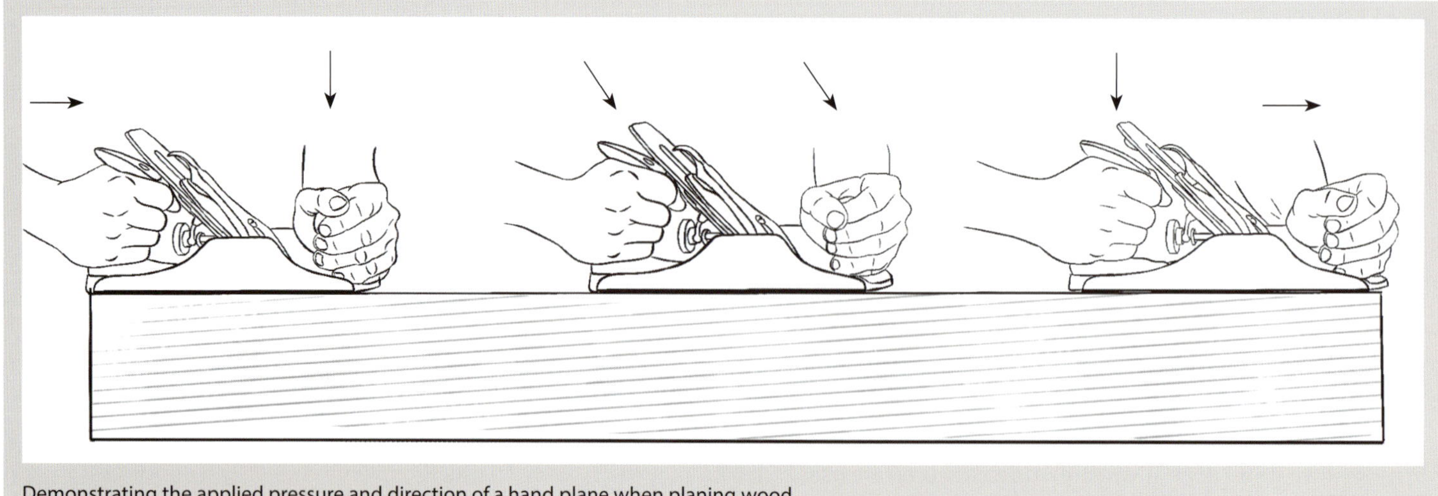
Demonstrating the applied pressure and direction of a hand plane when planing wood.

An 'f' is used to represent 'face side', which is your reference flat surface.

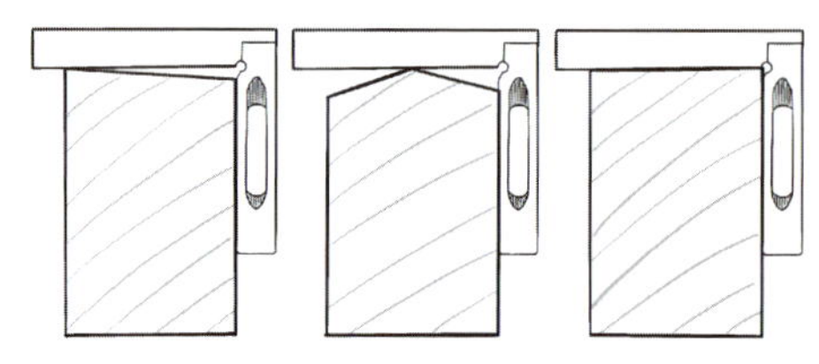
Left and middle: The edges are out of square and need planing. *Right*: An ideal surface, 90 degrees to the face side.

Another way of holding the plane when planing narrow surfaces is to pinch the front edge of the plane and guide it along the sides with your knuckles.

when deciding where to plane and sometimes by the end of it, your board will have shrunk substantially due to the planing process.

One of the main reasons why wood warp occurs is because of uneven drying and shrinkage. The following images show various ways that wood can warp.

When using the hand plane, start with more downward pressure on the front of the plane and a forward motion from the back of the plane. Transfer the pressure of the front hand to the back hand as you approach the middle of the surface. End off with more downward pressure on the back of the plane and a forward motion on the front of the plane. This transition of pressure and strength helps to keep your planing even and balanced throughout. If the pressure does not transit and remains at the front, then you will end up planing a slope. Once this surface is flat, label this 'face side', usually denoted with an 'f'.

Place the thicker part of the square against this surface and check the squareness of the edge.

In the above diagram the left and middle illustrations show that the wood is out of square and needs to be planed to achieve a 90-degree angle, as shown in the diagram on the right.

This will test your resolve in balancing the plane on this narrower surface. If you have a block plane, you can switch to one instead. Otherwise, another way of holding the bench plane is to pinch down the front with your left hand and run your fingers along the length of wood when planing.

If you keep getting a skewed angle you may want to: 1) Check the position of the blade on your plane, that it is set properly and parallel to the mouth of the plane; or 2) Adjust the pressure exerted on each plane stroke so that they are evenly distributed and not heavier on either side of your body.

Once this surface is flat and is 90 degrees to the 'Face Side', label this 'Face Edge' with an inverted 'v'. You now have two very important surfaces which you will take references from for the following steps.

Using a marking gauge, set it to the desired width. With the stock of the marking gauge against the face edge, scribe along the length of the wood. This will indicate the amount of waste you need to plane off and achieve the width you need.

Do the same with the last face of the wood for the desired thickness. Remember to always take reference from the face side and face edge.

If all the above stages were done correctly and accurately, then you will have successfully 'squared' a piece of wood. A simple test is to use a square

An inverted 'v' represents the 'face edge', which is your reference edge.

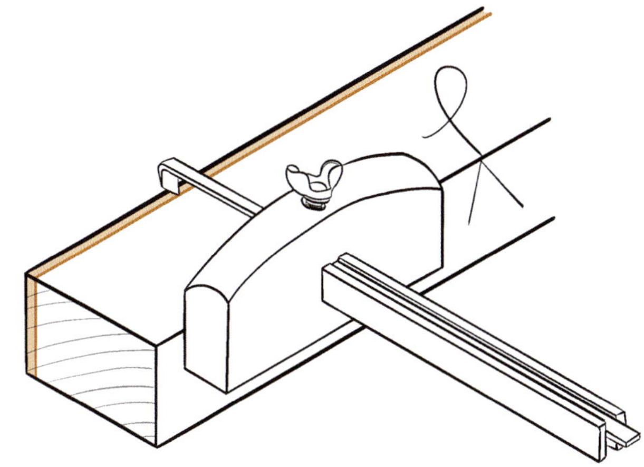
The highlighted portion indicates the area that needs to be planed to achieve the desired width.

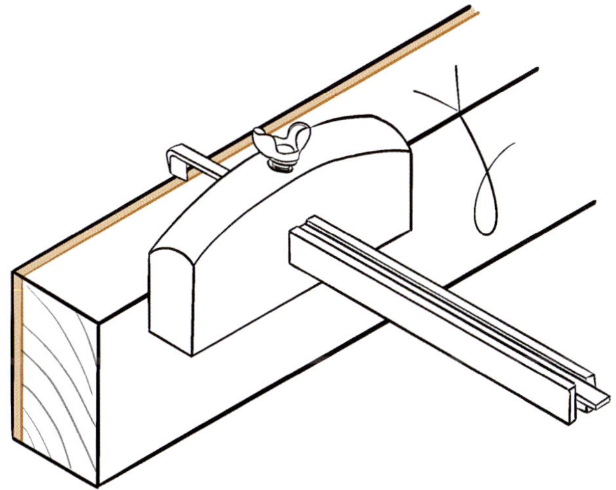
The highlighted portion indicates the area that needs to be planed to achieve the desired thickness.

It is good practice to always use the stock of the engineer's square on the face side or face edge.

and draw a line around the piece of wood with the following instructions.

1) Place the square stock on face-edge 'B' and mark across the face-side 'A'.
2) Rotate and place the square stock on face-side 'A' and mark across face-edge 'B'.
3) Place the square stock on marked face-edge 'B' and mark across 'C'.
4) Place square stock on the marked face-side 'A' and mark across 'D'.

Squaring off the end grain

One of the earlier challenges any woodworker will face is learning how to saw straight. More often than not, the saw will veer off the marked or scribed line and this is perfectly normal. It takes months or even years of practice to be able to saw in a straight line. For thinner boards, a shop-made shooting board can be used (*see* Chapter Eight). However, for thicker and larger material, a scribe-and-plane method can be used.

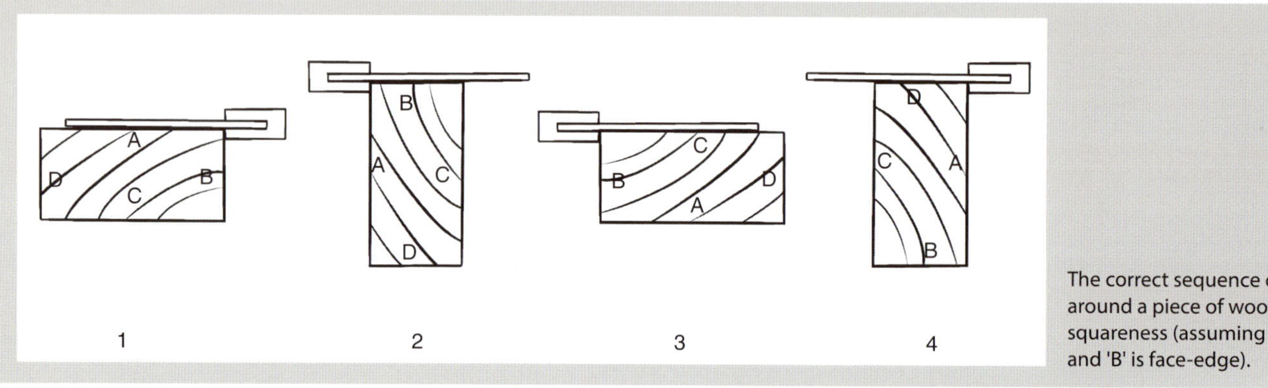

The correct sequence of drawing a line around a piece of wood to check for squareness (assuming 'A' is face-side and 'B' is face-edge).

The lines should meet up if the workpiece is properly squared and the correct way of using the engineer's square is applied.

SQUARING OFF THE END GRAIN

Being able to identify grain direction and to properly dimension wood is a basic skill that every woodworker should have. Once you are able to do both, you can then accurately prepare your materials for your projects, which is the start of any successful woodworking project. Using hand tools is a skill that will improve and grow over time. It just takes lots of practice and perseverance!

Use a marking knife to scribe a line around the piece of wood.

Use a block plane to chamfer the edges until it reaches the scribed lines.

Straighten the block plane and plane the end grain in portions until it is flat.

Using an engineer's square, check that all sides are properly squared.

THE SHOOTING BOARD

One of the most often-used equipment or jigs in the home workshop is a shooting board. It is used with a hand plane to make the edges of a board straight or trim off the end grain of a board. In a regular woodworking workshop, this is normally done with machines like the table saw or a mitre saw.

Depending on your skill level and experience, sawing wood will more often than not produce an uneven edge which is not precisely 90 degrees. One way to correct this is to manually scribe marking lines and then slowly plane down to these lines. While the scribe-and-plane method is often used when squaring larger pieces of wood, a shooting board will enable you to easily square off smaller and thinner boards easily and repeatedly.

A shooting board consists of two boards stacked together, with a perpendicular piece of wood acting as a fence to help hold the workpiece in place. A hand plane resting on its side is then used to repeatedly 'shoot' the ends off, gradually removing material to achieve a square edge. This fence also supports the end grain of the workpiece, minimising any chance of any end grain breakout.

A makeshift shooting board can also be made by stacking two shooting boards of different sizes on top of each other.

A shooting board mounted on the side of the workbench.

When two bench hooks are stacked on each other, they can be used as a shooting board.

From left: A no. 5½, no. 5 and no. 4½ hand plane, with the shooting board as a comparison of size.

A hand plane being used on the shooting board to square up the end grain.

In fact, some woodworkers simply use a bench hook as their shooting board directly on the workbench.

As with all home-made woodworking jigs, there are many designs to choose from with different features and additional attachments. The example shown here is a basic one featuring a moveable fence that can be adjusted whenever it gets worn out through repeated use. It can be used clamped on a worktop, pushed against some bench dogs or fence, or have a bottom fence installed to be pushed against from under the worktop.

You will need two pieces of manufactured boards like plywood or MDF to form the base and the raised platform. The base should be sturdy and thick enough to remain flat, roughly 12mm–18mm (½–¾in) thick. It should also be long enough to accommodate the length of your hand plane. In this example, It fits a no. 4½, no. 5 and no. 5½ hand plane.

The purpose of the base is for the hand plane to slide forwards and backwards while the step is a raised platform for the workpiece to sit on. You will also need a piece of wood as the fence and some hardware to hold the fence down onto the plywood.

On the sole of the hand plane, there is a mouth where the blade protrudes out and a roughly 6mm border on its sides where the body of the plane extends down. This is where the hand plane takes reference from when sliding to and fro. Therefore, the thinnest material that should be used for the raised platform should be the same or more than this border.

A close-up view of the mouth of the handplane, showing the distance of the blade from its sides.

Cutting List for Shooting Board

Part	No. of	Length	Width	Thickness	Material
Base	1	400mm (15½in)	300mm (12in)	15mm (⅝in)	Birch Plywood
Upper Platform	1	400mm (15½in)	200mm (8in)	15mm (⅝in)	Birch Plywood
Top Fence	1	210mm (8¼in)	40mm (1⅝in)	35mm (1⅜in)	Pine
Bottom Fence (optional)	1	200mm (8in)	40mm (1⅝in)	35mm (1⅜in)	Pine

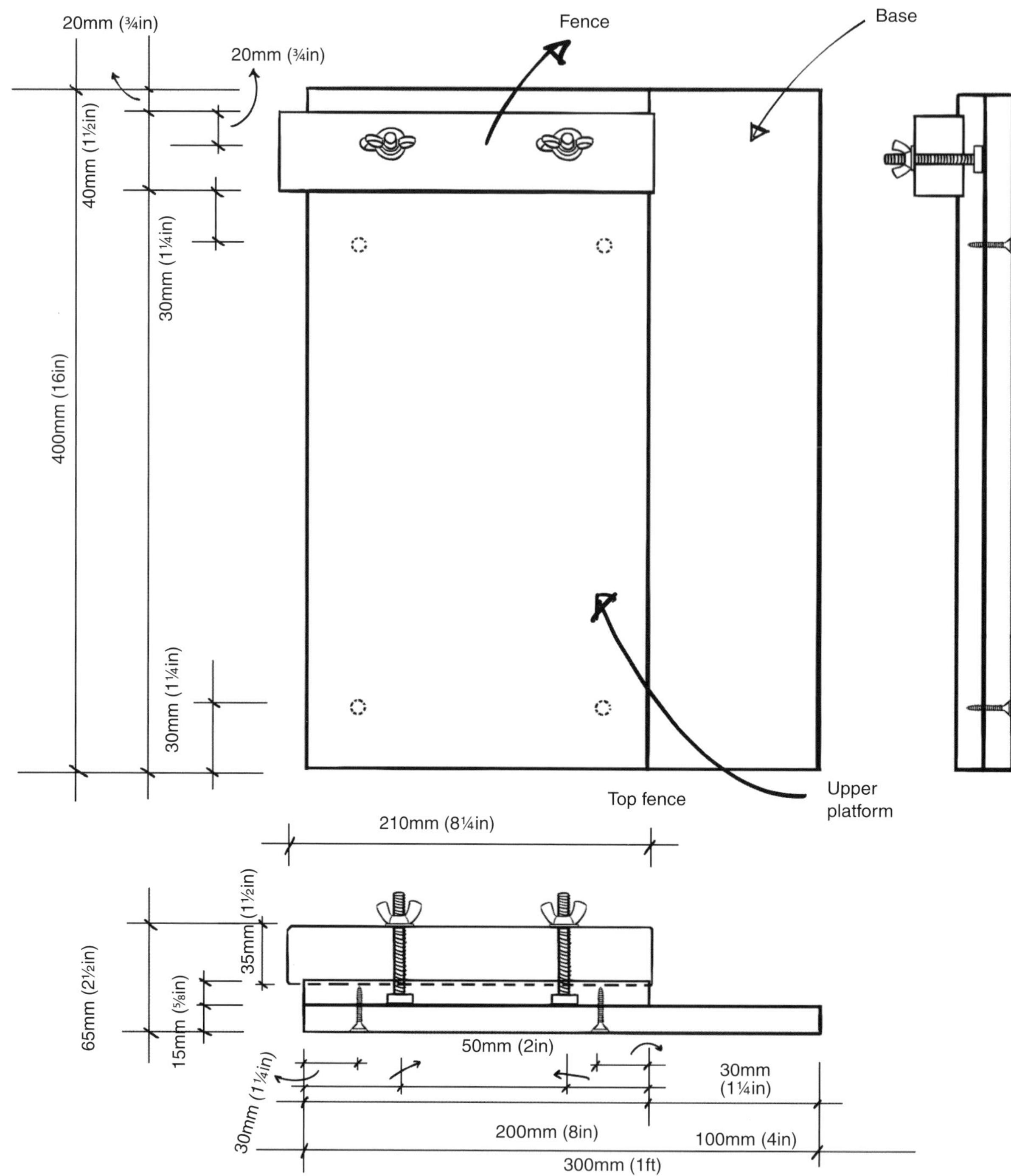

Illustration plan of a shooting board.

MAKING A SHOOTING BOARD

Measure and cut your materials to size. The upper platform should be wide enough for your hands to hold down the workpiece. The shooting edge of the upper platform should be planed straight, as this will be the reference for the plane.

After placing the upper platform on the base, the area for the hand plane should be wide enough to accommodate your hand plane while on its side. The fence should be high enough to hold the workpiece, but should not be taller than your hand plane, as it will interfere with the shooting process.

Place your fence around 20mm (13⁄16in) from the top edge of the platform and make sure it is squared to the inner platform. Having this extra space in the front of the fence gives the plane a little more reference surface so it remains straight after cutting.

With the position of the fence fixed, use a marking knife to scribe the width of the fence. For a tighter fit, scribe a slightly narrower width, allowing trimming to achieve a more precise fit.

Create a 2–5mm (1⁄16–¼in) shallow housing to accommodate the fence by using a shoulder or router plane. An option is to use an electric router with a straight bit. Once the housing is created, dry fit the fence and check for squareness.

To affix the fence to the upper platform, the hardware required is a pair of hex head bolts, washers and winged nuts. The length of the bolt should be more than the combination of the upper platform and the fence.

Measure the width and thickness of the hex head (12mm/½in wide and 5mm/¼in) thick) and diameter of the threads of the bolt (7.74mm/5⁄16in). This is to determine the sizes of the drill bits to use to make the necessary holes.

On the bottom of the upper platform, drill the larger hole to a depth of 5.5mm (¼in) for the hex head. Switch to a smaller drill bit and drill through the upper platform aligning with the centre of the larger hole. Insert the hex bolts and trace out the shape of the hex head using a pencil.

Use a chisel to trim the recess to accommodate the hex heads. Gently tap the bolts in from the bottom of the upper platform and check that the heads are flushed with the platform and do not freely rotate.

Remove the bolts. Using the upper platform as a guide, place the fence slightly proud of the shooting edge and drill the corresponding holes through the fence. Reinsert the bolts. The fence should sit secured in the housing.

To allow for adjustment of the fence, drill two or three more holes to elongate the opening for the bolt. Using a marking gauge, scribe along the length of the opening and use a chisel to clean up the waste.

Insert the bolts without the fence, then screw the upper platform onto the base from the bottom. Using a finely tuned hand plane, trim the shooting edge of the platform till no more shavings appear.

Insert and position the fence so that it is flushed and squared with the shooting edge of the platform. If It is out of square, remove the fence and trim the misaligned surface until it is correct.

Rub some wax on the surface of the base to allow smoother movement of the plane. You can screw on an optional bottom fence to act as a hook to be pushed against the worktop when in use.

There are many modifications and additions in the construction of a shooting board. Here are a few examples:

- A shooting board with a sloped platform. This allows the plane to perform a skewed cut, which can produce a cleaner cut and also utilise more portions of the plane blade.
- A shooting board with a Teflon sheet to aid in the gliding motion of the plane. This shooting board also features a piece of polycarbonate strip under the upper platform to act as a guide for the plane.
- A ramp attachment also known as a 'Donkey's Ear'. This helps in trimming vertical mitres.
- A 45-degree triangle that helps in trimming horizontal mitres.

SUMMARY

The saw and hand plane are essential tools for dimensioning timber. Accurately squaring the material is even more crucial before the start of any projects. Even a millimetre of inaccuracy in a piece of wood will be compounded into a large gap later on. Understanding how to read the grain direction of wood and the proper use of a square to true up a piece of wood is the start of a good foundation of woodworking. In addition, making your own jigs will help improve accuracy and repeatability as you begin making your own projects.

A sloped or ramped shooting board.

A shooting board with a white teflon sheet and polycarbonate strip for a smoother movement of the plane.

A donkey's ear ramped attachment is used to make 45-degree mitre cuts.

A 45-degree jig is being used on the shooting board to trim 45-degree edges.

Laying out your tools is useful to visually decide what to include in your toolbox.

CHAPTER 7

MAKING A TOOLBOX

You now have your set of tools and have spent considerable time preparing them. Now is the time to make a home for them. As mentioned previously, a good set of tools will last a long time and having a place to store them is one of the best things you can do for them. My first toolbox was a cardboard box with everything lumped into it. It was messy, things were clanging around and was simply unsightly. I then acquired a cheap handyman toolbox, but my tools were still very much in a mess and it was difficult to organise anything in it.

I have to admit that a couple of years into my woodworking life, I splurged and bought myself one of those metal rolling tool cabinets with multiple drawers. It keeps everything organised and can be pushed around if I need to. However, these cabinets are not cheap and can take up a substantial amount of space. This worked for me, as by this stage I had accumulated a considerable number of tools and needed a large enough storage space for all of them. However, as a beginner with a small set of tools, this might be an overkill.

A HOME FOR YOUR TOOLS

A simple and beautiful Japanese-style toolbox is a good starting point for your tools. It is elegant and easy to make with simple tools. I feel that it is a personal sense of achievement to make a purposefully designated storage place for the very tools that support you in this craft.

DESIGNING YOUR TOOLBOX

Rather than give specific dimensions and sizes, I would much prefer to guide you in how to plan and decide the right size for your toolbox. I cannot expect you to have the exact same tools as me, so once you get your set, you can start deciding on designing your own toolbox.

The first thing you would need to do is to decide what you want to include in your toolbox. As much as you would like to fit everything into the box, you have to be realistic and practical in this decision. For example, it would not make sense to build a 1.5-metre toolbox just to fit a 1 metre ruler in.

Next, lay all your tools out on a surface and see how they can be split into various categories. For example, putting larger and bulkier items like your planes and marking gauges as one group, and flatter, smaller items like measuring tools into another group, and so on.

For my toolbox, I have decided to split them into these three sections:

- Planes, hammers and marking gauges
- chisels
- measuring tools and stationery

I decided not to include my hand saws and intend to hang them off my workbench as I use them quite often. But they can still fit into my toolbox if I detach the blade from its handle. Incidentally, I have a Japanese foldable saw that fits nicely into my toolbox in the folded position.

The next step is to decide the outer dimensions of the box. Do you have a specific area where you want to place this toolbox? Or is there a space on an existing shelf that you would want the toolbox to sit on? If there is a particular area you want the toolbox to sit in, then you will need to work backwards from that dimension. If not, you can continue to design one as you would to accommodate your tools.

For the main lower-part of the toolbox, I will put a no. 4½ hand plane, a block plane, a shoulder plane, a pair of marking gauges and a hammer. I will then make a chisel tray to accommodate all my chisels, and finally an upper tray for my measuring tools.

I start by physically laying out my tools on the floor and using some masking tape to mark out the overall dimensions; much like creating a floor plan for my toolbox. A great and reusable way to visualise the size of the toolbox is to make use of cardboard or paper to cut out the sizes of your tools in different views; top-down, sideways, and

What better way to start your woodworking journey than with a home for your tools?

Using masking tape to set an area helps to position where the tools can potentially go within the box.

Using paper templates of your tools allows you to easily position them over the floorplan.

maybe even from the back. Then, on your floor plan, you can start shifting them around to see how they can fit within the given space. This helps me get a sense of what the toolbox will look like and whether I have enough space for the items that I want to fit in it. Remember to consider the thickness of your wood stock at this point, because a 230mm-wide box suddenly shrinks to less than 200mm of internal space after subtracting the amount of space the wood itself takes up.

After arranging where I want things to be, I set the length to 520mm (20½in), the width to 230mm (9in) and the height to 200mm (8in), which brings me to the next step: deciding what material I should use. The toolbox should be sturdy due to the weight that it will be carrying, so consider thicker material for the main structure. You may choose a hardwood such as ash or oak, depending on your skill level, but I would recommend a softer wood like pine or poplar for a beginner. You might outgrow this toolbox in the future as you acquire more tools or streamline your tool selection, so I would choose a more budget-friendly material for your first toolbox.

With the dimensions of my toolbox set, I am ready to draft out my drawing. This will include front, side and top elevations. It will be helpful to write notes on what kind of joints you intend to use and how certain parts will come together.

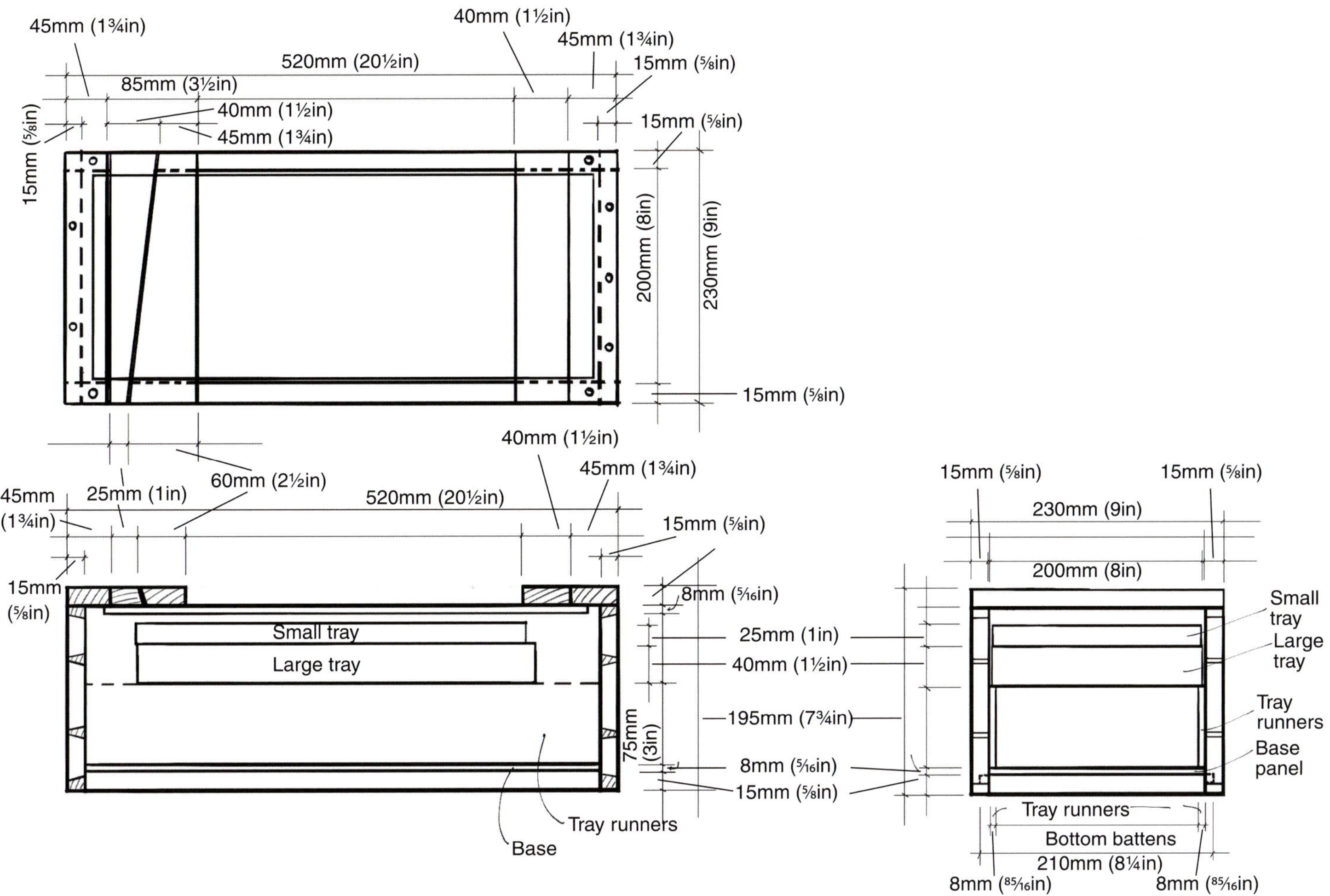

Illustration plan of the toolbox.

Cutting List for ToolBox

Part	No. of	Length	Width	Thickness	Material
Long Sides	2	520mm (20½in)	180mm (7in)	15mm (5⁄16in)	Pine
Short Sides	2	220mm (8¾in)	180mm (7in)	15mm (5⁄16in)	Pine
Bottom Battens	3	216mm (8½in)	80mm (3⅛in)	15mm (5⁄16in)	Pine
Top Battens	2	230mm (9in)	45mm (1¾in)	15mm (5⁄16in)	Pine
Base Panel	1	490mm (19½in)	200mm (8in)	8mm (5⁄16in)	Pine
Lid Panel	1	460mm (18in)	200mm (8in)	8mm (5⁄16in)	Pine
Lid Fixed Batten	1	230mm (9in)	40mm (1⅝in)	15mm (5⁄16in)	Pine
Lid Locking Batten and Key	1	230mm (9in)	80mm (3⅛in)	15mm (5⁄16in)	Pine
Tray Runner Inserts	2	490mm (19¼in)	75mm (3in)	8mm (5⁄16in)	Pine

PREPARING YOUR MATERIAL

JOINING BOARDS

It is not easy to get boards that are wide enough for your projects. You can always join boards to achieve the width you need. Since I already have boards of 15mm (⅝in) pine that are 90mm (3½in) wide, by joining two boards together I will get 180mm (7in) wide boards to start with; which was roughly the width I needed for this project. The first thing is to inspect them visually and if possible, line up the grain direction. This helps with planing them flat after they are joined.

Once you have decided on which boards are to be joined together, draw a triangle to mark their orientation. The edges need to be prepared so that both boards will be straight and aligned when joined together. This is exactly the same process as when squaring edges, as described in Chapter Five. The most ideal situation is when all sides are squared in perfect 90-degree angles to achieve a very perfect joint.

Another way of joining boards is to plane the edges slightly bowed in the middle, so that when both edges come together, the clamping pressure on the sides will cause the middle to be naturally clamped tight. This may reduce the number of clamps you need.

A small paint roller is an efficient way to apply glue on large surfaces. You can use a plastic container with a lid to hold a reservoir of glue and store the roller when it is not in use. It is important to make sure that there is sufficient glue along the edges before putting the boards together and starting the clamping process. I like to start from one end, making sure that with every clamp I tighten, I use my hands to feel if the boards are aligned properly.

Depending on how long your boards are, you will need a certain number of clamps to hold them together while gluing up. As I am joining boards to 520mm (20½in) long, I decided that I needed about three clamps to help keep the clamping pressure consistent. I like to have clamps alternate on the bottom and the top to maintain an even pressure throughout the boards. If you are joining longer pieces, more clamps should be used to balance out the pressure across the entire length.

A method to make sure that the boards remain flat while glueing up is to clamp additional battens on the top and bottom. Do make sure to put some parcel tape on the surface of the battens to reduce the likelihood of them getting stuck to your workpiece.

Some woodworkers insist on cleaning up all the excess glue that gets squeezed out, while others leave it and remove the dried glue after. I tend to wipe off what I possibly can with a dry cloth first, then a damp cloth and then remove the rest after the glue dries.

Lay out your materials and mark the orientation you want them joined.

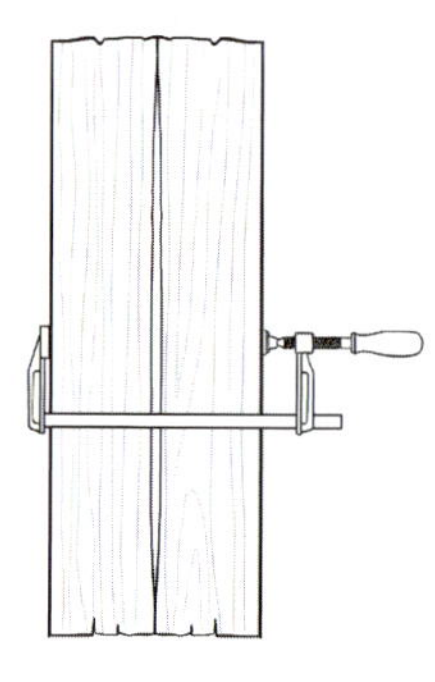

Clamping boards which are purposely made with a slight bow in the middle (exaggerated).

Paint rollers are great for flat surface glue ups for even and consistent spreading of glue.

When glueing-up panels, alternate your clamps on the top and the bottom to provide even pressure.

Flattening the boards

Once the clamps are removed, I use an old chisel to remove the bigger bits of dried glue. I then use a ruler to check the flatness of the joined boards. Sometimes, due to unforeseen movement during the clamping process, one side might end up higher than the other, so this is the time to bring out the hand plane to flatten the boards.

Start by using your plane to plane the surface diagonally across the grain. Do it for a few passes and you can very quickly see that the higher spots start reducing and slowly meet with the lower parts. Continue to use a ruler to check for flatness at each section of the board. Eventually, the board will be flat and you can straighten your plane and take straight passes. Sometimes I switch to a block plane to take very light shavings to clean up the board. It is important to be consistent with the motion and pressure of the hand plane. Sometimes we can get carried away and end up with a board sloping at the ends or the sides, or having one board thinner than the other because of over-planing. Always check as you go along.

With the boards all joined and flattened, lay them out and mark-out where you will need to cut. Ideally all the boards should be of the same thickness, but it really is okay if they are just slightly off; no point pulling your hair out and getting frustrated trying to get them to exact thicknesses.

For my tool chest, I needed two longer pieces of 520mm (20½in) and two shorter pieces of 230mm (9in). I usually give myself an allowance of about 6mm (¼in) for any sawing inaccuracies or 'accidents', so I marked out 525mm (20¾in) and 235mm (9¼in). After sawing the boards to my required lengths, I squared up the sides by planing the end grain upright. To reduce the risk of breakout at the end, you can either make a small chamfer or clamp a piece of wood at the end of the board.

All four pieces of wood required for the main carcass of the toolbox are now prepared and the next step is labelling them. Marking out and labelling your work pieces is a very personal thing; some woodworkers use numbers and alphabets, whilst some use short phrases and even symbols. There is also the cabinetmaker's triangle, which has been used for centuries. Eventually you will find your own way to label them efficiently for your working process. I also like to use arrows to identify their upright positions and mark out whether they are inside or outside facing. As much as I can, I like to place them in their correct orientation to visually inspect how everything looks when I label the pieces.

To start building the box, the four sides need to be joined together to form its basic structure. I would like to introduce a common corner joint; the dovetail joint. Many beginners shy away from attempting dovetails, as they seem very complicated to do. I beg to differ and feel that it is a great joint to learn and through it, to begin understanding wood joinery.

Use a straight edge to check for the evenness and flatness of your boards after each glue-up.

Start with diagonal passes followed by straight passes to flatten boards.

It is important to label all your components and their orientation so that you can visually identify where they belong.

MAKING THE TOOLBOX

There are countless methods for marking out dovetails. Some woodworkers prefer to have equal spacing dovetails of the same size while others prefer a mix of different sizes to have an interesting detail. I like to keep it simple. First I decide how many tails I want but usually keep it to an odd number (you will find out why). For this tool chest, I have decided to have three tails. To save marking out (and cutting time), you can tape both of the longer boards together orienting them with their outside faces facing outwards. This is a method I adapted to make things quicker by 'killing two birds with one stone', cutting two tails at a go.

1 MARKING OUT AND CUTTING THE TAILS

Tape and clamp both long sides upright in your vice. To mark the dovetail positions, measure from one edge 10mm (⅜in), 50mm (2in) and 55mm (2¼in). This will create the markings for the first tail, the first pin, and the edge of the middle tail. Do the exact same markings from the other edge. You now have the markings for your three dovetails.

Set ten degrees on the bevel gauge using a protractor as the dovetail angle. Place the bevel gauge using the pencil lines as a guide and mark out the face side. Alternate the bevel gauge so that the ten-degree lines should be converging at the tails instead of the pins.

Set your marking gauge to the thickness of the short side of the box. Scribe a line on the pins and mark an 'X', as this is now the waste that needs to be removed. Run the marking gauge a few times to achieve a more pronounced and visible line that will be helpful during the clearing out of waste.

Tilt and secure your boards with the tails aligned to 90 degrees to your workbench. This means that instead of tilting your saw, you just need to focus on sawing straight down. Keep the workpiece as close to the jaws of the clamps as possible to ensure stability.

Keeping your saw in the 'X' zone, follow the pencil lines and saw till you reach the scribed lines. This ensures that the material removed is from the waste portions. Cut all the lines which have the waste on the right side before flipping the board around and doing the same for the other side.

Use a fret saw to remove the waste between the tails. Slide the fret saw blade down the tail line from the previous step. Ease the fret saw blade slowly rotating it from a vertical to a horizontal position. Rotate the work piece perpendicularly and saw off the half pins on the ends.

Separate the boards. Using the same marking gauge settings, scribe a pronounced line over the pins on the inner face. This will clearly define where the shoulder lines are, making it easier to clean up the joints with a chisel later.

To trim off the sides, start by paring from the middle until you reach the shoulder line. Trim off the sides with an outward slicing motion. A pushing motion might crush the end grain fibres. Use a square to check if the shoulder is flat and clear of any debris in the corners.

Lay one side of the workpiece onto a waste board. With the chisel upright, pare gradually towards the shoulder line. In most circumstances, this is normally done by hammering the chisel with a mallet. This quieter method of paring the waste slowly is more suitable for apartment woodworking.

Alternatively, clamp the workpiece vertically with a piece of wasteboard behind to reduce the likelihood of any breakout. Slowly trim towards the shoulder line ensuring that the pin socket is flushed. A bevel-edged chisel works really well to clean off any debris at the corners.

DOVETAIL ANGLES

There are inexpensive dovetail markers with various angles that you can buy. Or you can also make your own dovetail markers fixed at a certain angle so you do not have to repeat the protractor and bevel gauge step each time you make a dovetail. An angle between 7 to 12 degrees (Fig. A) is well accepted in the realm of dovetailing. Anything less than 7 degrees (Fig. B) will have too little mechanical strength and an angle of more than 15 degrees (Fig. C) will be too extreme and may have unsupported end grain at the tips which will snap easily.

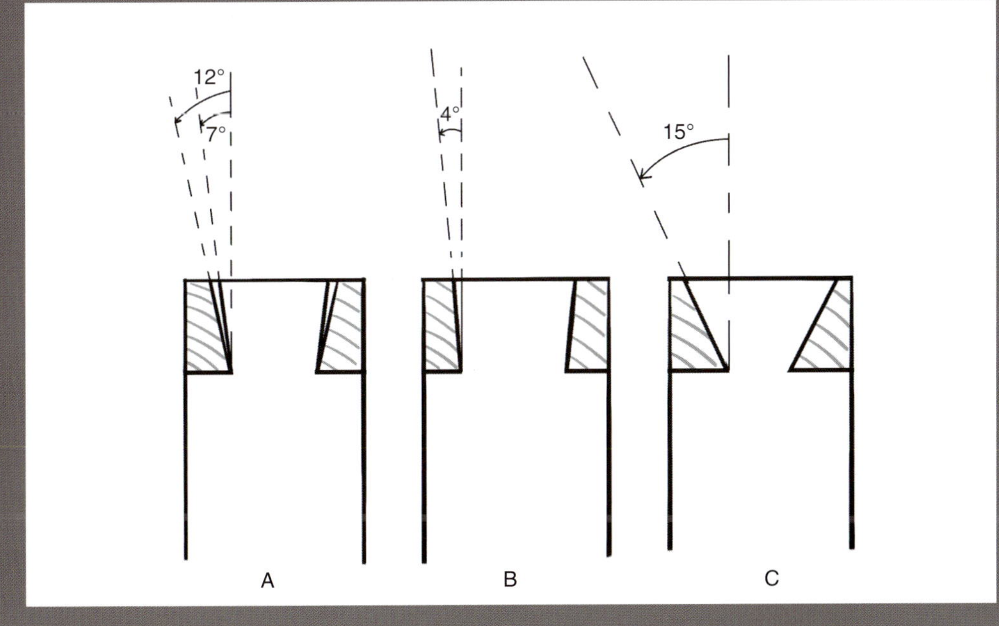

Illustration showing different dovetail angles.

2 MARKING OUT AND CUTTING THE PINS

Clamp one short side board vertically. Then place its corresponding long side board (marked with the same letter) with the tails perpendicular to its end grain. Weigh it down so that it will not move while transferring the markings. Make sure that the ends of both boards are aligned and straight.

Use a knife to score the outline of the tails onto the end grain of the short side board. Start with a light cut, then repeat the process a few times for a more pronounced line. A useful tip is to tilt the knife at both ends of the cut to slightly mark the face sides so that the markings can be easily transferred later on.

Set a marking gauge to the thickness of the long board and gently scribe to indicate the shoulder line. With a small square and a knife, match up the markings at the end grain to the shoulder line. Start with light strokes with the knife to avoid accidentally veering off with the wood grain, then add pressure to achieve a more defined marking.

Label the waste with 'X'. Use the marking gauge to score a more pronounced shoulder line at the areas that are to be removed on both sides. You will notice that the lengths of the marking lines are different on the inside and outside faces due to the shape of the tails.

Remove the waste between the pins. Start with the vertical cuts following the angle that is marked out on the end grain that corresponds to the tail. Note that when you complete the cut horizontally with a fret saw, the widths on both sides of the board are different due to the taper of the tail.

Clean up the waste with a chisel. Using a square or a ruler, make sure that the end grain of each joint is straight. If the square or ruler is rocking and does not sit flush, this means that the joint will not fit properly when assembled. Continue to trim down the excess with the chisel.

Dry-fit each joint individually and trim down as necessary. Once they all fit snugly, you can join them all together. If you feel too much resistance and friction when fitting the joints together, it means that more trimming is required. Do not force the joints or the wood will split.

The basic carcass of the box is now complete. Once assembled, if there are any slight differences in height, use a block plane to trim the edges down. When trimming, work gradually, as removing too much material on one side can result in a slanted box.

MAKING THE BASE FOR THE TOOLBOX

There are several ways to make a base for the toolbox. The following are some ideas for attaching bases. The simplest way is to screw a panel from the bottom. I almost never use this method, as all the weight from the box is being pulled downwards, placing all the stress on the screws themselves. Perhaps I am just being paranoid and should have more faith in screws, but I always prefer to use more form of interlocking joinery, especially when there are gravitational forces at play.

For this toolbox, I chose to use three battens attached across the width of the box supporting a thinner base panel. The base is not glued in place and will allow for movement during seasonal changes. The battens will be secured using a barefaced tenon to the longer sides of the toolbox.

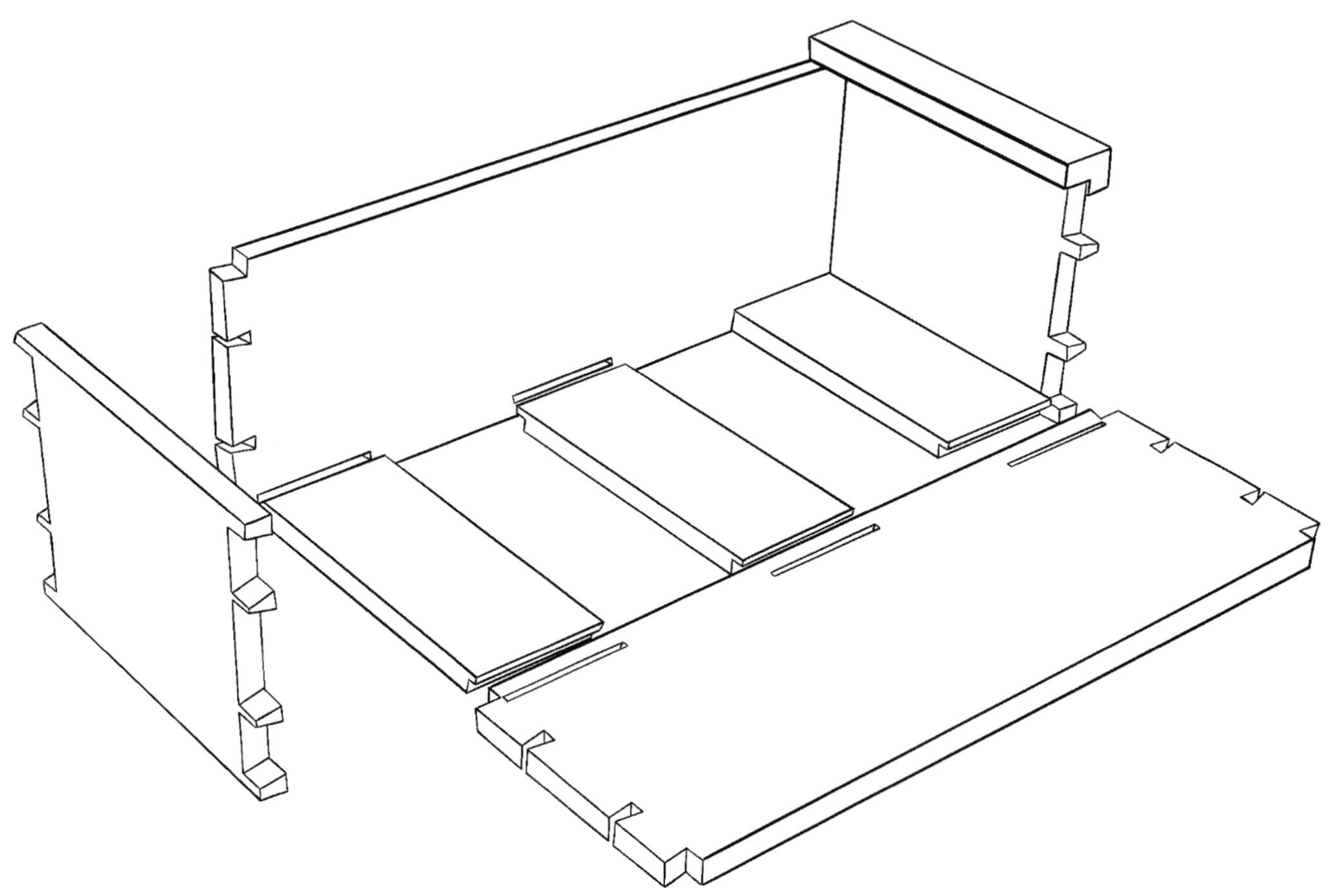

An exploded view of how the bottom battens are installed. These three battens will support a panel of wood as its base.

3 MAKING THE BASE

Prepare three battens. The three battens will be attached to the sides of the carcass using the mortise and tenon joint. (*See* Chapter Eight – Barefaced Tenon.) The tenons will be inserted to about half the thickness of the sides. In this case, the internal width of the box is 200mm (8in) and the thickness of the long sides are 15mm (⅝in), which means the length of the battens should be 200mm + 7.5mm + 7.5mm = 215mm (8½in).

Place the three battens and mark their lengths on the long sides of the carcass. Set the marking gauge to the thickness of the battens to mark out the upper position of the mortise. In theory, the length of each mortise is the full width of each batten (80mm/3⅛in), the width of the mortise is half the thickness of the batten (7.5mm/5⁄16in) and the depth is half the thickness of the long side (7.5mm/5⁄16in).

Set the marking gauge to half the thickness of the batten to scribe the lower position of the mortise. To make the mortise, use a 6mm (¼in)drill bit. Mark out the depth of 7.5mm (5⁄16in) by using a piece of masking tape on the drill bit. Align the drill bit in the middle of both scribe lines and drill consecutive holes to the required depth. Remove most of the waste using the drill before cleaning up the rest with a chisel.

Using a marking gauge, set the dimensions from the edge of the long side to the bottom of the mortise and transfer the measurements onto the end grain of the battens. Similarly, mark out the length of the tenon based on the depth of the mortises you have made. Saw off the waste marked 'X' and clean up with a chisel or shoulder plane.

Tenons can be cut slightly oversized and slowly trimmed for a good fit. Depending on the type of wood you use, some woods can 'compress' slightly to achieve an even tighter fit. If you have accidentally over-cut your tenons, you can use some thin veneers to fill up the gaps.

Piece together the carcass with the base battens and measure out a suitable panel for the base. This can be a thin panel of solid wood or any type of manufactured boards like plywood. In this example, an 8mm-(5⁄16in)-thick jointed pine panel is trimmed and fitted into place.

MAKING THE LID OF THE TOOLBOX

The Japanese-style tool chest has a clever way of locking its lid in place with a simple locking mechanism. The lid is slightly longer than the opening after the lid battens are attached. The lid slides in from either side and once it is in, slides towards the opposite direction. When it hits the stopper on the lid, both ends will be tucked under both battens preventing it from coming out. A key is then slid in, locking the lid in place.

Here is an illustration of how it works:

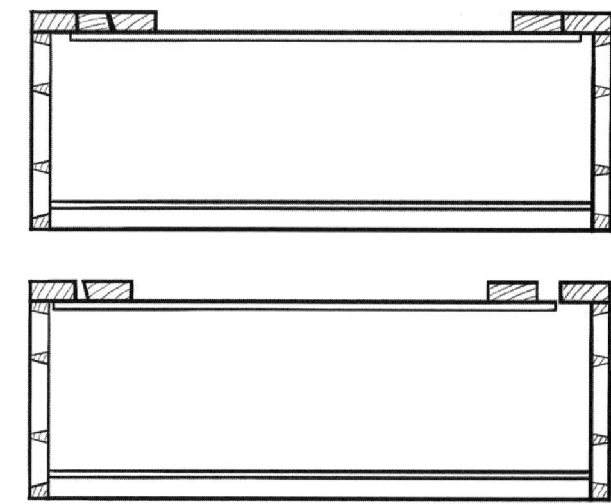

The locking key is removed and the lid is slid towards the left. This releases the lid from the top battens.

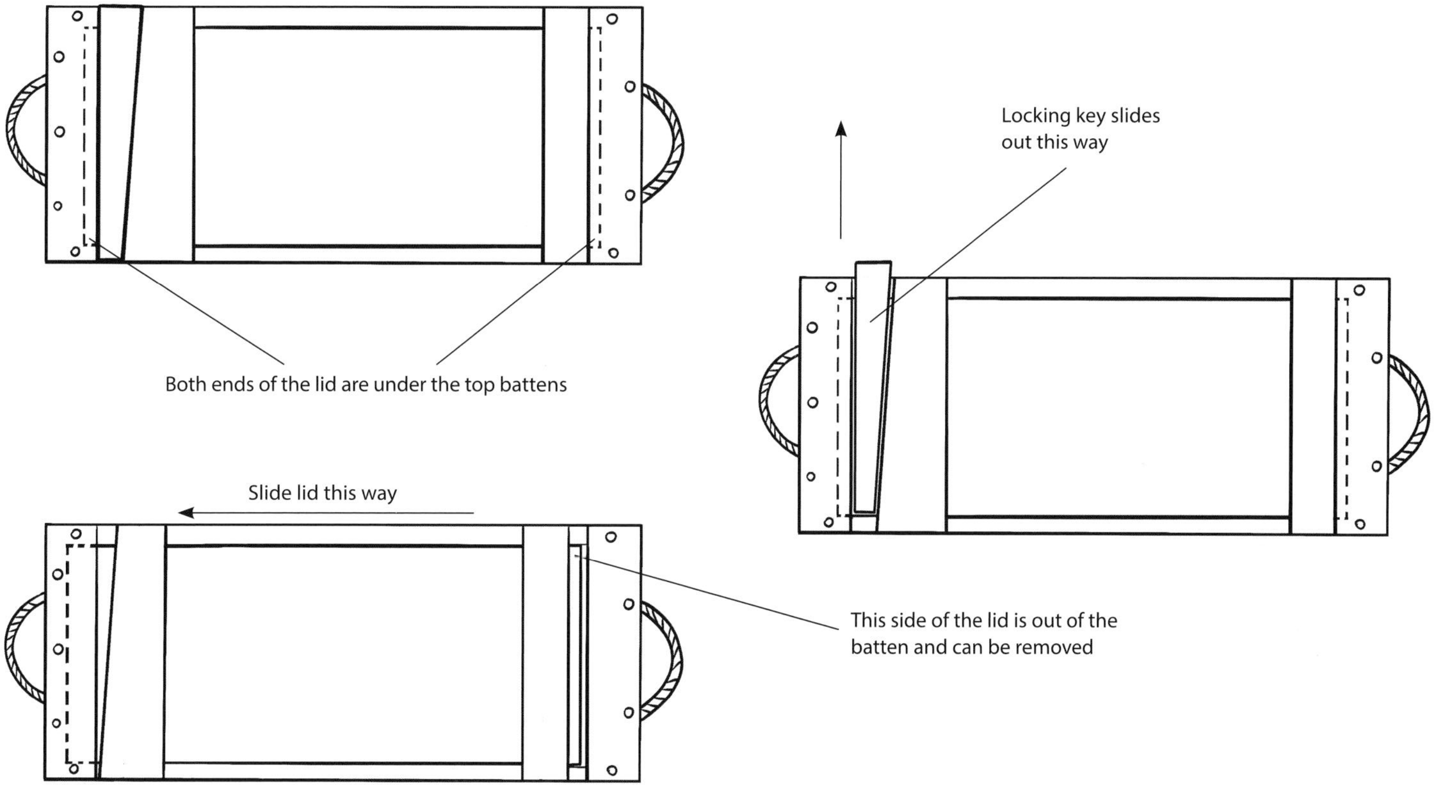

Both ends of the lid are under the top battens

Locking key slides out this way

Slide lid this way

This side of the lid is out of the batten and can be removed

Top: Lid is closed and locked; *Middle*: Locking key is removed; *Bottom*: lid is unlocked and slid towards the left to be removed.

4 MAKING THE LID

1

Cut two identical pieces of wood for the lid battens. These two battens will hold the lid down and lock it into place. You can pre-drill the screw holes with a slightly deeper and wider hole to be plugged later on. I like to mark one side differently with an extra hole as a personal preference to know the direction of the box.

2

Hold both the lid battens with clamps while you measure and cut a panel for the lid. One side of the lid will have a stopper that is screwed in from the bottom. Use some double-sided tape to test and see what the optimal distance from the edge of the lid this stop should be.

3

The other side of the lid houses the locking mechanism. Start by cutting a piece of wood diagonally to create two parts: one will serve as the locking fixed batten, while the other will act as the moveable key. They can have a slightly angled profile to help keep the key locked in place and prevent it from falling out (using the same principle as the dovetail).

4

Secure the locking batten to the underside of the lid with screws. Shape the key to fit snugly into the locking area, allowing smooth movement while maintaining a secure hold when engaged. Now the box is complete and the fun part begins by customising the inside!

CUSTOMISING THE BOX FOR YOUR TOOLS

There are countless ways to organise and position your tools into your toolbox. If you have done initial drawings, there is already a rough placement for everything to follow. I like to create sections and dividers so that the tools do not bang against each other, especially for the larger items like hand planes.

Making trays

For this toolbox, I designed two trays: a shallower one for measuring tools and a deeper one for chisels. Both will be made in the same way for joining the sides but I will show two different ways of attaching the bases.

Trays are great to organise your tools and keep them neatly separated.

Different sets of tools may require different ways of separating and storage.

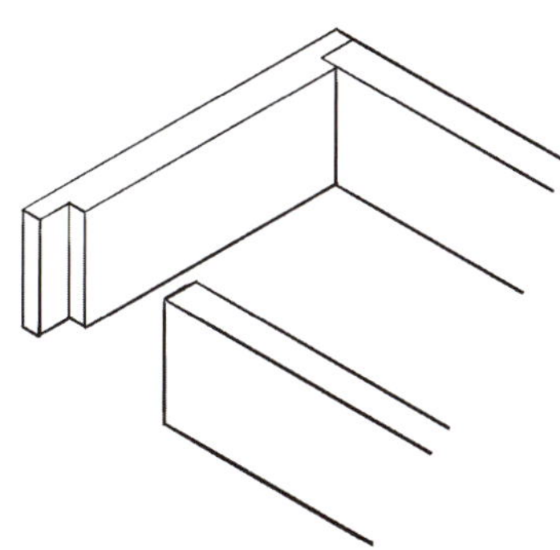

A rebate is cut onto the shorter sides to accommodate the longer sides.

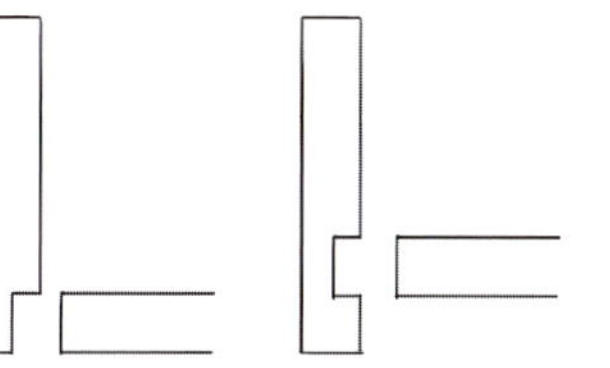

These are two basic ways of attaching the base to the trays.

Cutting List for Trays

Part	No. of	Length	Width	Thickness	Material
Lower Tray Long Sides	2	375mm (15in)	40mm (1⅝in)	8mm (5⁄16in)	Pine
Lower Tray Short Sides	2	200mm (8in)	40mm (1⅝in)	8mm (5⁄16in)	Pine
Upper Tray Long Sides	2	370mm (14¾in)	25mm (1in)	8mm (5⁄16in)	Pine
Upper Tray Short Sides	2	200mm (8in)	25mm (1in)	8mm (5⁄16in)	Pine
Tray Bases	2	375mm (15in)	190mm 7½in)	8mm (5⁄16in)	Pine

5 MAKING THE TRAYS

Prepare the parts for the trays – the shorter ends should fit into the internal width of the box, while the longer sides should be less than the internal length of the box. This allows for easy placement and removal of the trays. On the short ends, use a marking gauge to mark out the thickness of the long sides and cut into about halfway through to create a rebate joint.

One method of attaching the base to the tray is using a groove. The tray base is a 4mm- ($\frac{5}{32}$in)-thick plywood. This can be done by marking out the grooves with a marking gauge and slowly chiselling off the waste. Similarly, you can use a plough plane with a blade of the same width or an electric router with a 4mm ($\frac{5}{32}$in) bit.

Alternatively, the base to the tray can be attached with a rebate as shown at the bottom of the picture. However, take note that this method of attaching the base to the tray sides is determined by the strength of the adhesives used. This means that the tray will not be able to withstand heavy loads.

End grain adhesion is notorious for failure. Prior to gluing up at end grains, it is advisable to first prime the end grain with a dilute PVA mixture of 1:1 PVA and water. This allows the mixture to penetrate and prepare the surface. Allow it to dry for at least fifteen to twenty minutes before the actual glue-up later.

Rubber bands are very useful clamping devices. I like to find various sizes of rubber bands to accommodate different objects. You can also use clamping blocks to increase the tension as well as a downward pressure for adhesion of the base to the rebate joint. Make sure the trays are square before leaving them to dry.

Once the trays have been glued together, trim off any protruding parts and clean off any dried glue. The tray should fit into the box loosely. To support the tray, cut two boards to serve as tray runners. Their height should be slightly above the tallest item stored beneath.

On the short sides, measure and drill two holes to attach rope as carrying handles. Any type of thick rope will do. Do this above the tray runners as the knot behind can help prevent the trays from banging against the sides of the box.

This larger tray holds my chisels and some other items. To organise the space efficiently, you can cut and glue dividers to create sections within the tray. All items should sit in the tray without protruding as the smaller tray will be stacked on top.

SUMMARY

There are lots of ways to customise your toolbox or modify it internally to fit different types of tools. I use some smaller pieces of wood to make up sections or dividers so the tools do not knock against each other. As you grow or outgrow this toolbox, you can always configure it differently for various other uses.

A home for your tools.

A Roman fresco in Pompeii depicting a carpenter at work while seated on a low workbench.

CHAPTER 8

YOUR FIRST WORKBENCH

Why is a workbench called a workbench when most of the 'workbenches' we see are really tables? According to Roger B. Ulrich's book *Roman Woodworking*, a fresco found on the wall of the House of Vettii, Pompeii, shows an ancient woodworker in a seated position working over a low bench. In *The Workbench Book* by Scott Landis, a drawing based on an oak plank found in Saalburg, Germany in 1934 dating ca. 250 BC bears certain hallmarks of a workbench. Some believe that this discovery is an early example of a Roman workbench.

A WORKBENCH OR WORK-TABLE?

Several images from *Das Hausbucher der Mendelschen* (*The Nuremberg House Books*) – a manuscript spanning 1425 to 1806 – contain illustrations depicting various other craftsmen working on low worktops supported by sawhorses, suggesting that a bench was also commonly used alongside taller surfaces.

Even in the East, traditional Chinese and Japanese woodworkers still work in a seated position, usually on the floor or on a low type of staked bench as their ancestors would have done. So perhaps while a lower bench was the first type of woodworking worktop, it has gradually evolved into the taller, table-like type of workbench we see and use today.

In fact, making a modern version of a staked workbench is a great idea for a beginner woodworker in an apartment. It can have all the components used for woodworking but can also remain as part of your home furniture. If you are unsure about making a full-sized workbench due to the space it takes up and also the amount of material it requires, then a Roman-style workbench might be a good option for you. The basic design of the Roman-style workbench is a sturdy top with four legs in a slightly splayed angle. Splayed legs offer stability and support as compared to having the legs stuck in at a straight right-angle. I made one myself following a very informative instructional video by Christopher Schwarz.

However, even after building a Roman workbench, I often found myself going back to using that old IKEA shelf. The Roman workbench is great and can be modified to suit many types of woodworking, but one thing that annoyed me was the wasted space below it. I then wondered if

A Roman-style workbench with an additional vice at the end.

A hybrid workbench that features some storage solutions.

The overhang is useful for gripping onto your workpiece when sawing and clamping longer pieces for ripping.

I could merge the Roman workbench with the storage solution of the shelf....

The result was this hybrid 'workbench' that actually can be a shelf when standing upright but is designed to be used when lying down on its side – very much like the IKEA shelf. However, there are various reasons why I designed it this way. The overhang on one side is useful for gripping onto your workpiece when sawing. It also serves as a clamping point if you need to secure your workpiece to the bench, especially when you are ripping longer pieces of wood.

The narrower opening is a space to slot your bench hook and smaller jigs. The middle area has a backing that is slotted in with the help of grooves and helps with any racking movement. This space is also a compartment to store my toolbox as well as my Moxon vice. On the other end is an additional storage space but it can also be a possible installation point for a vice. The surface can be left as it is or have holes drilled to accommodate bench dogs or plane stops.

This hybrid workbench can be made easily by screwing the parts together or in my case, I spent some time creating grooves for the dividers to sit in before screwing them in. These grooves do not have to be very deep and can be made with a combination of chisels and a router plane or shoulder plane in the absence of an electric router. The grooves help with the overall stability and will help when assembling the parts together.

This style of workbench, like the Roman-styled workbench, is designed to primarily be used whilst seated especially when planing smaller pieces of wood. It also makes use of your body weight and even your legs for holding your workpiece whilst sawing.

However, I understand that not everyone is familiar with working whilst seated and it can also be rather awkward to some of you. So, through my journey of woodworking I have designed a regular standing workbench suited for an apartment woodworker.

There are many styles and types of workbenches, each with their different purposes and usage. A quick search on the internet will show countless designs ranging from historical reproductions to modern bespoke ones that look too good to be used.

Ripping a plank of wood using the knee as a clamp.

*The Anarchist Workbenc*h by Christopher Schwarz has in much detail classified different types of workbenches and Lon Schleining's *The Workbench* is an excellent resource for making various types of workbenches.

The following are the main components for a typical woodworking workbench when considering the type that is suitable for you.

- ***The Bench Top*** The bench top (or worktop) is the surface you will work on. Bigger is better in most cases, but that may be a challenge in a small apartment. Measure your space accordingly before committing to the size of your bench top. An ideal bench top should be strong, sturdy and heavy. Common bench tops are made of maple, beech and oak, and sometimes, manufactured boards like plywood. However, if you are a beginner, it would be wise to use something a little more manageable to work with. Softwoods like pine and spruce have been used for bench tops and can also be quite cost effective. Ask your local timber yards what they have ready-stocked, as this can reduce the cost of milling from rough boards to custom specifications. This is just a way of using what is first available before needing to mill more material.

- ***Feet or legs*** Once you have a working bench top you can either use it as it is on an existing surface, or you can make some feet or legs for it. The height of the workbench is another highly debatable subject. For most Japanese tools, this will normally be a lower workbench; elevated slightly off the floor using low sawhorses, requiring you to be often on your knees. For using Western-styled planes, the worktop will need to be higher at around the hip or around the knuckles when standing up.
- ***Vice*** A vice to secure your work down is usually one of the first attachments. It is important to be able to clamp your workpiece firmly onto the workbench before being able to work on it effectively. However, installing a vice can be a daunting task. There is always a fear of misalignment or drilling holes that are not perfectly straight. So before attempting to install a store-bought vice, do try out a few clamping ways with just the use of f-clamps, as mentioned in Chapter Five.

The type of workbench is very personal and it is also determined by the kinds of tools you have.

A torsion box-style worktop (*top*) and a laminated solid worktop (*bottom*).

There are many types of vices. Some are designed to be used at the ends of workbenches while others are used in the front.

Workbench Accessories

A plane stop is necessary to hold or 'stop' the timber from moving forwards (or backwards if you are using a pull-type of plane). Plane stops can be built directly into the bench top, or made as separate attachments. There are also ready-made stops which you can buy that can help you with this operation.

The easiest way to make a makeshift plane stop is to clamp a strip of wood across the bench top, keeping in mind that this strip of wood should be thinner than the workpiece you intend to plane so as not to obstruct the plane when planing.

Bench dogs can also be used as stops for planing and other holding purposes. There are ready-made ones, or you can also consider making simple ones out of some wooden rods. They can also be used in combination with some wedges to hold your work down.

There are also many types of vices and clamps and accessories which you can use with the workbench. It will be easy to fall into the rabbit hole of spending countless hours just looking for that perfect workbench to build. There is no shortage of videos and magazine articles enticing you with easy-to-build and quick beginner options to make a workbench. All of which may suit you. There is no easy answer to the question of which is the best type of workbench. Ultimately, it will depend on what kind of woodworking you do. Do not let this dissuade you from building a workbench. Even making a basic one is a learning experience in woodworking on its own!

A removable plane stop is simple to make and can be used across multiple work surfaces.

Bench dogs can be used with wedges for holding workpieces.

THE APARTMENT WORKBENCH

Traditionally, a stable, heavy and large workbench is desired for woodworking, but as an apartment woodworker, I needed to balance mobility, stability and compactibility of my design. This workbench that I designed and made for my own apartment space is based on a trestle-style workbench with some slight variations on the bench top. Since I mainly make boxes and smaller furniture, I do not need (or have the space) for a large bench.

I have included two bench top versions: 1) A laminated solid bench top made by laminating several beams of wood to form a solid worktop; and 2) A torsion box-style bench top made by using a frame construction and a plywood (or solid) worktop.

While it may look strange at first glance with the odd shape of alternating wood beams in the middle, this is specifically designed for an apartment workshop and can be easily modified to suit different types of woodworking. The end with the outer protruding beams acts as a quick vertical clamping point and the recessed area can be a mounting point for a small router table in the future. On the other end, the narrower width can be an accessory attachment point for other jigs like a bench hook (*see* Chapter 5) or a shooting board (*see* Chapter 6).

This workbench is designed to be compact, easy to build and can be suited for woodworking in an apartment.

This protruding beam serves as a clamping vice to hold your workpiece.

The recess can become a mounting point for a removable router table in the future.

This end of the bench top can be a mounting point for a bench hook and other jigs.

A LAMINATED SOLID BENCH TOP

This laminated solid bench top consists of multiple beams of wood joined width-wise to form a thicker and sturdier worktop. Arranging one-metre beams in this manner also increases the general length of the worktop slightly.

Of course, if you prefer a regular rectangular bench top, simply join and glue the multiple beams together uniformly and plane it flat after.

I am using radiata pine with the dimensions of 75 × 35mm (3 × 1⅜in). You can use other species such as maple, beech or ash, which are commonly used for bench tops. The length of the worktop should be dictated by the space available to you. The timber yard which I purchased them from had lengths of about 2,140mm (7ft), which yielded slightly over 1,000mm (40in) when cut in half.

The width of the bench top is dictated by the material you can get. In this case, by joining nine pieces of wood, thickness-wise I will be able to get a table width of 315mm (12½in). Joining lesser beams in the other orientation is also possible, but will result in a thinner bench top.

A laminated solid bench top is simply made by joining multiple beams of wood.

Cutting List for Laminated Solid Bench top

Part	No. of	Length	Width	Thickness	Material
Bench top	9	1,000mm (40in)	75mm (3in)	35mm (1⅜in)	Pine

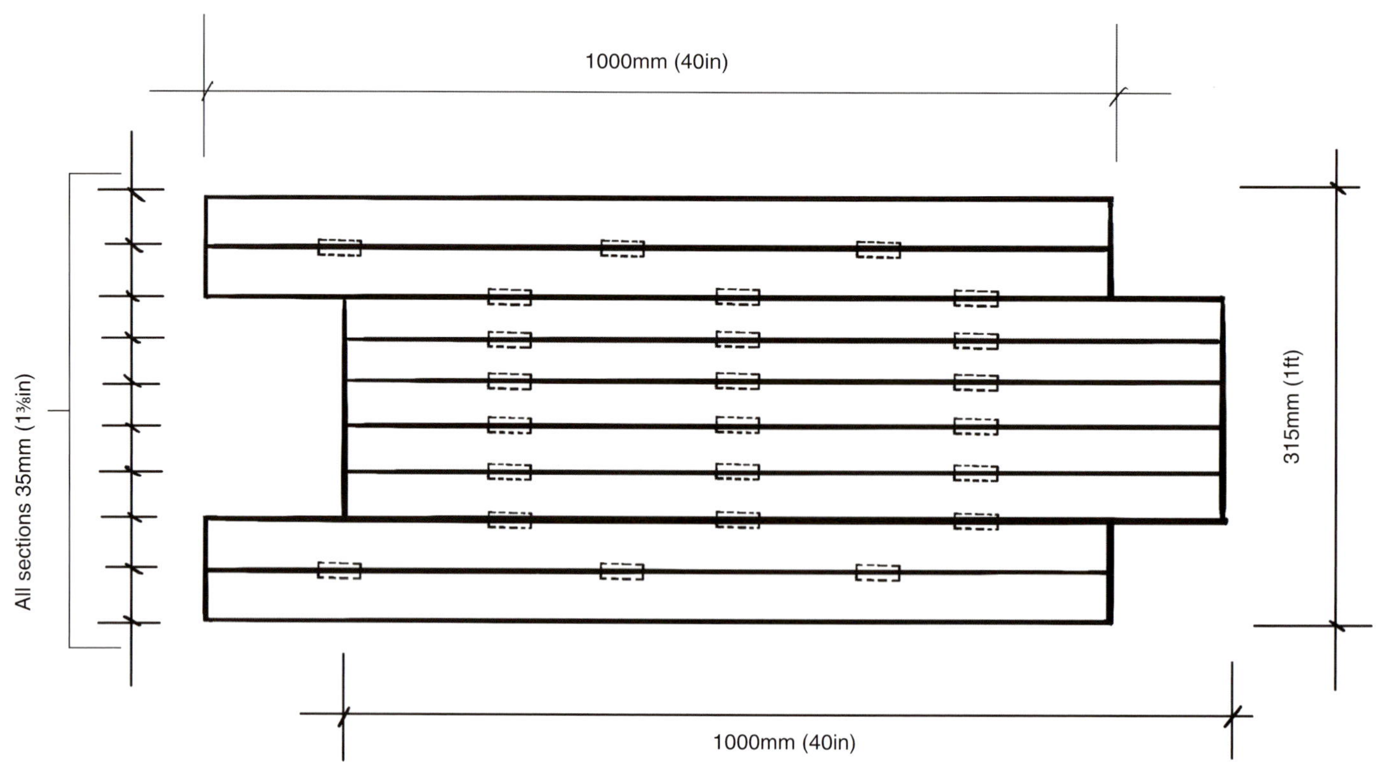

Illustration plan for making a laminated solid workbench.

MAKING A LAMINATED SOLID BENCH TOP

Lay the beams out to visually check the size of the resulting bench top. Place the outer pieces in pairs and group five beams to make up the middle part. The ends are not trimmed off and are left as is at this stage.

The beams can be glued together directly or by using the help of loose tongues in the middle (*see* box below). Once glue is applied on both surfaces, align and clamp them up. I use a paint roller to apply adhesives on large surfaces.

Joining them in pairs is easier than trying to glue them all at one go. Slowly build up the middle group and trim off the ends before attaching the outer pairs. This is the part where you can decide if you want a traditional rectangular worktop or to offset it by 150mm (6in) according to this design.

If you do not have wide enough clamps, use a ratchet or a combination of masking tape and heavy items to weigh it down. Once joined, check the surface for squareness and plane flat. The laminated bench top can be used as a removable attachment to an existing table or legs can be made for it.

MAKING AND USING LOOSE TONGUES

Loose tongues or 'splines' are basically pieces of wood glued into mortises or stopped grooves and can be used as locators when glueing up. They also help hold both mating parts in place as the glue tends to make them slide around during the clamping phase. I like using thin strips of plywood as my tongues, as they are of uniform thickness and are made up of layers of wood in alternating grain direction. For example, if I am using 6mm- (¼in-) thick plywood, I can then use easily available 6mm drill bits or a 6mm router bit to create the mortises for them. You can also use any solid wood offcuts and make them into tongues. They have to be in the short grain orientation, meaning the grain direction is running along the length instead of the width. The power tool equivalent is a biscuit jointer or a domino joining machine.

Use a marking gauge to mark out the positions of the mortises. Remove most of the waste using a hand drill before cleaning up with a chisel. You can also use a router with a fence for this. The mortises do not have to be exactly the width of the tongues. They can be slightly longer so that there is some wiggle room when aligning them during the glue up. They also do not have to look pretty as they will be covered up and totally unseen after glueing up. The one important point is to make sure that they are deep enough to accommodate the loose tongues, otherwise both mating parts will not meet at all.

Loose tongues can be made in batches from long strips of solid wood or plywood.

A TORSION-STYLE BENCH TOP

This second option uses less material by following the idea of a torsion box with an attached plywood top as the worktop. It is generally a frame construction with one or more middle cross supports. As compared to a solid worktop made from laminating several pieces of wood together, this method uses less material and is relatively lighter. The trade-off is a less dense top which does not take the impact of hammering very well. But since this book is exactly about reducing the use of hammers, it can be well considered for an apartment worktop. As with the first design, the worktop does not cover the entire surface, allowing one end to have exposed beams to serve as vertical clamping points in the absence of a proper vice.

The frame can be attached simply with some screws, but this is an opportune time to introduce some interlocking joinery. This design requires corner joints and some cross supports. The single finger joint and the single dovetail joint are great first corner joints to learn and either will be suitable for this. For the cross supports, the mortise and tenon joint and the dovetail housing joint will be introduced. You can choose to mix and match these joints based on your preference and skill level.

The size of this worktop can be modified based on your requirements and space. For my worktop, I decided on a length of 1,000mm (40in) and a width of 320mm (12½in).

Decide on your dimensions and cut out the parts needed. I always lay them out and label each piece for easy reference later on. When deciding the lengths of the cross supports, always work from your internal dimensions, then add the lengths of your tenons to it. For example, if the internal width is 250mm (9¾in), and my tenons are 20mm (¾in) each, then the length of each of my cross supports should be 250mm + 20mm + 20mm = 290mm (11½in).

A torsion box-style bench top is made with various joinery to form a frame supported with cross supports.

A piece of plywood or jointed solid wood can be installed as the surface.

Laying out your rough cut pieces and labeling them will help you in orienting all the parts visually.

Cutting List for Torsion Box Style Bench Top

Part	No. of	Length	Width	Thickness	Material
Long Sides	2	1,000mm (40in)	75mm (3in)	35mm (1⅜in)	Pine
Short Sides	2	320mm (12½in)	75mm (3in)	35mm (1⅜in)	Pine
Cross Supports	3	290mm (11⅜in)	75mm (3in)	35mm (1⅜in)	Pine
Top	1	765mm (30¼in) or 1,000mm (40in)	320mm (12½in)	15mm (⅝in)	Pine

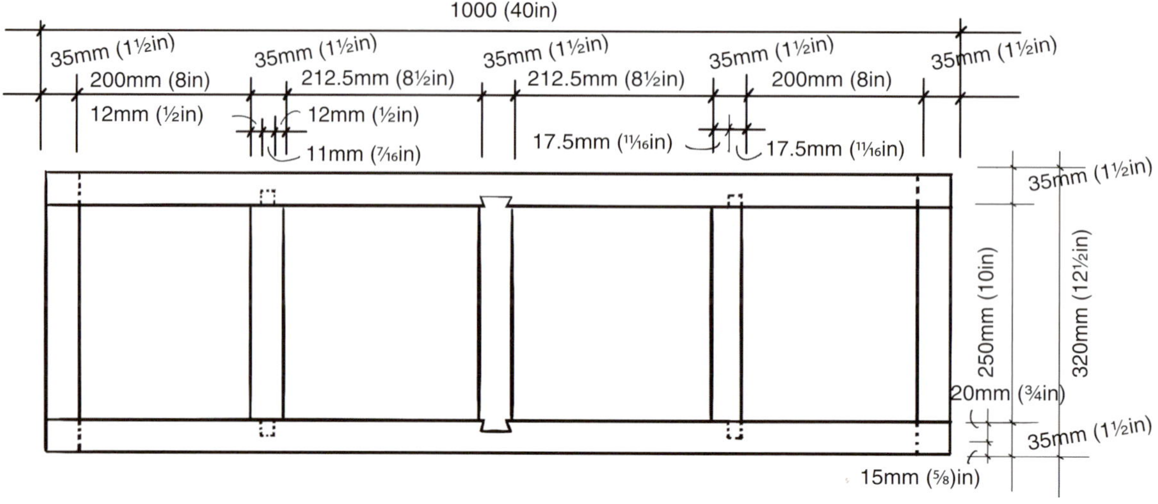

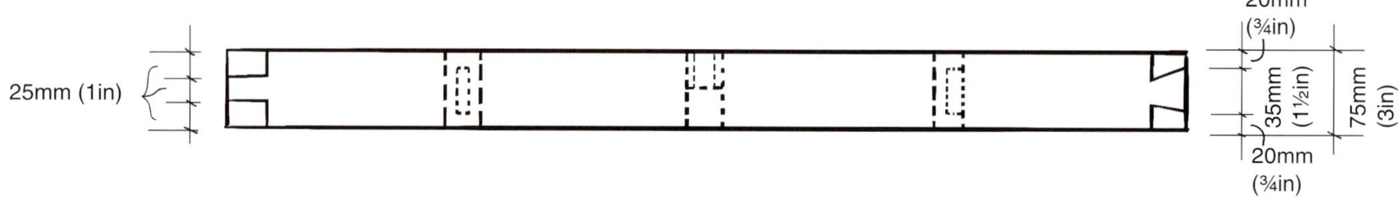

Illustration plan for a torsion-style worktop.

TWO BASIC CORNER JOINTS

The first two basic joints we will be using to make the outer frame are the single finger joint and the single dovetail joint.

The single finger joint is an easy first joint to attempt. It has a good amount of surface area for glue and is easy to clamp up. The difficulty increases with the number of fingers within the joint.

If you would like to challenge yourself, the single dovetail joint is a great introduction to dovetails. This joint has an added mechanical strength because of the shape of the interlocking tails.

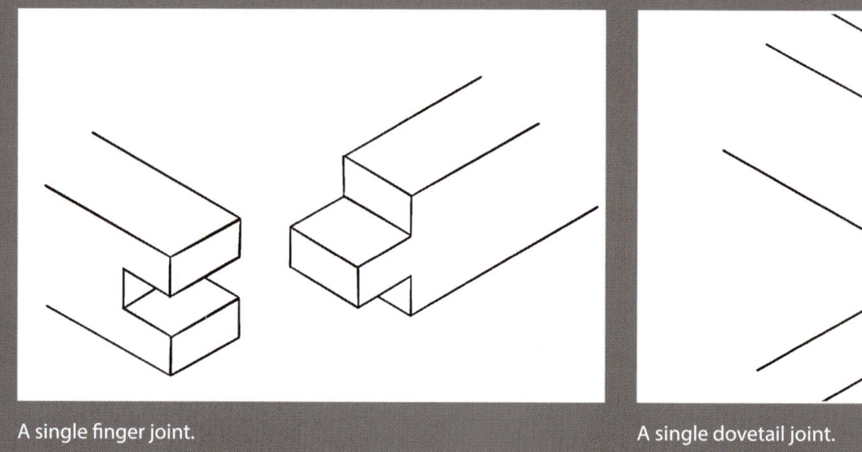

A single finger joint.

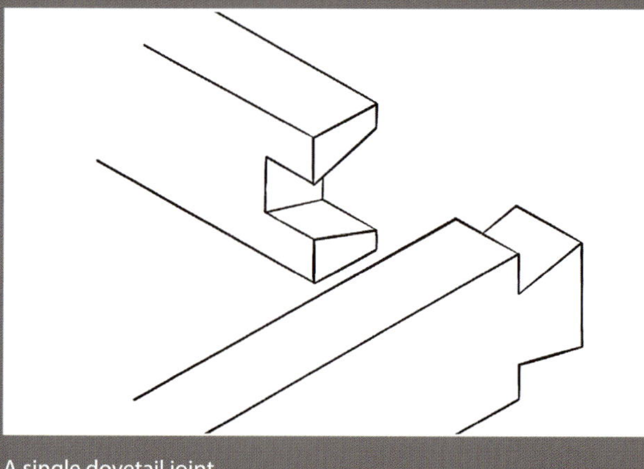

A single dovetail joint.

TORSION BOX-STYLE BENCH TOP 1 – MAKING THE FRAME

1

Set your marking gauge to the thickness of the sides and scribe onto the edges using the end grain as reference. This marks the depth of the joint and establishes the shoulder line. Do this lightly on all sides.

2

To make the 'finger', measure the width of the sides and divide it by three. You can set your marking gauge and scribe this out, indicating the waste area with 'X', making sure to keep your saw within this area.

3

Secure your workpiece on your worktop. Follow the line and start sawing at a forward angle towards the shoulder, keeping the saw well in the 'X' area. As you are reaching the shoulder line, finish off vertically.

4

If you have accurately cut within the lines, the same measurements can be used on the short sides. If not, place the long side over the short side and transfer the markings with a marking knife.

5

Transfer the knife marks onto the face side towards the shoulder line. Follow the line and start sawing at a forward angle towards the shoulder. Remove the waste between the joints with a fret saw and clean up the joint with a chisel.

6

Fit the joints together. If they are too tight, trim the joints to fit. If they are too loose, you can consider increasing the thickness by gluing some wood veneer or thin strips of wood to the finger.

Set your marking gauge to the thickness of the sides and scribe onto the edges using the end grain as reference. Set your bevel gauge or use dovetail templates to mark out your tails. I measured about 20mm (¾in) from the sides, roughly dividing into thirds.

Follow the line and saw off the waste, keeping your saw within the waste area. Try to sight both the lines on the face and end grain when sawing to maintain a straight cut. Start sawing at a forward angle before ending off in a vertical position.

Clean up the shoulders and the sides of the tail with a chisel. The inner sides of the tail should be perpendicular to the face so that it can be inserted between the pins without wedging itself too tight or ending up having large gaps.

Place the tails over the end grain of the short side, making sure they are perpendicular to each other. Transfer the shape of the tail with a marking knife. Start with light strokes gradually to eventually get a more pronounced marking.

Transfer the knife marks towards the shoulder using a small square and further redefine the shoulder marks with the marking gauge. Remember to label 'X' on the portion you need to remove.

Remove the waste and fit the joints together. If the joint is too tight, trim the joints to fit. If it is too loose, consider glueing thin strips of wood and trim to fit again. With both ends complete, you can start working on the cross supports.

MORTISE AND TENONS

Mortise and tenons are widely used in woodworking for joining two pieces of wood, often at a right-angle. In its simplest form, the tenon side which has the protruding part will meet with the mortise which has a slot cut into it. There are many versions of the mortise and tenons, each having their respective applications. The shoulders around the tenons generally absorb racking forces and also conceal any imperfectly cut mortises.

Here are two versions of the mortise and tenon joints used in this project. Both will be cut 'blind', meaning they will not protrude through. Prepare your mortises first, as it will be easier to cut your tenons to fit into them rather than the other way round.

Barefaced Mortise and Tenon (3 shoulders)

The first version is the barefaced mortise and tenon with three shoulders. This joint has one side without any shoulders, making it easier to align with the mortise on the frame.

Shouldered Tenon (4 shoulders)

On the other side, a fully shouldered tenon is used. Marking this tenon out requires some additional mathematics. Unlike the barefaced tenon which starts exactly on the side of the cross support, this tenon has shoulders on both sides. This means that you need to account for additional material on each side when making your measurements.

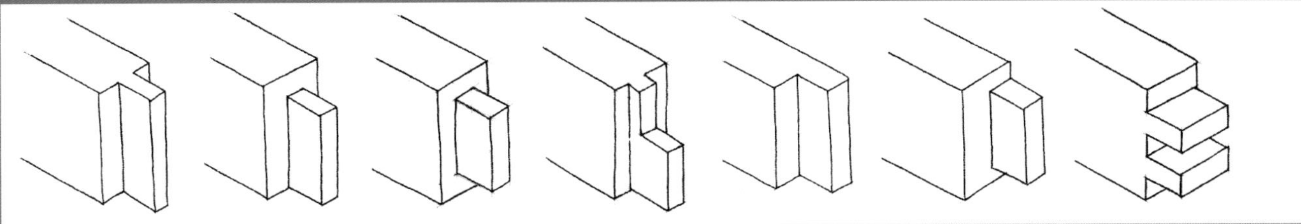

From left to right: standard tenon with two shoulders, tenon with three shoulders, tenon with four shoulders, haunched tenon, barefaced tenon, barefaced tenon with shoulders, twin tenons.

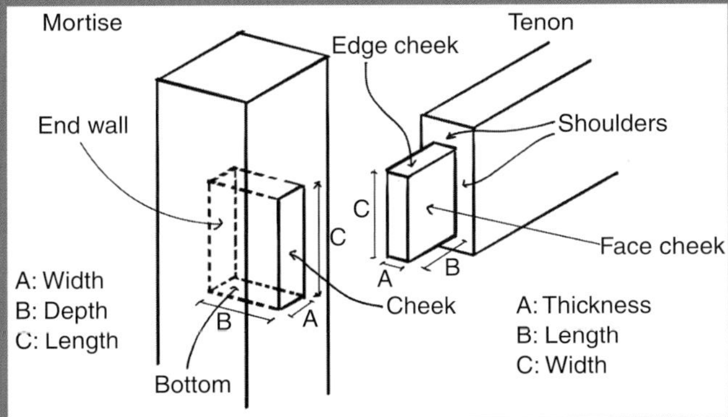

The mortise and tenon joint, with its terminology.

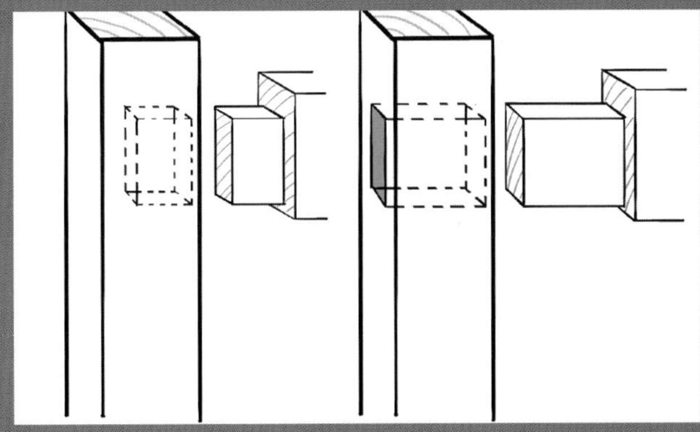

A blind (*left*) and a through (*right*) mortise and tenon.

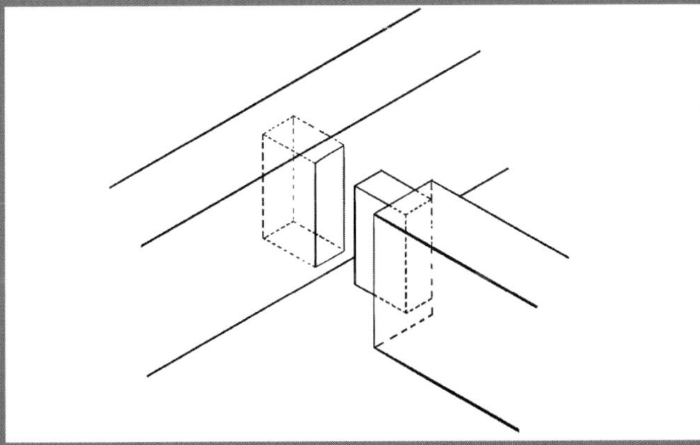

A barefaced mortise and tenon (three shoulders).

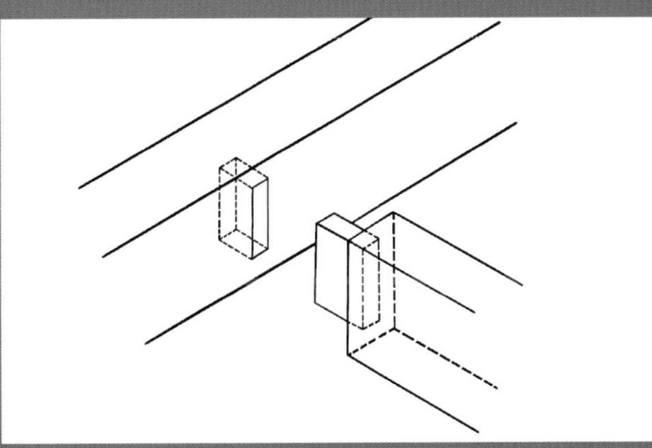

A fully shouldered tenon (four shoulders).

TORSION BOX-STYLE BENCH TOP 2 – MAKING THE CROSS SUPPORTS

Start from the shoulder line of the corner joints and measure 200mm (8in) inwards for the start of the mortise. The mortise width is half the width of the cross supports (17.5mm/¹¹⁄₁₆in), and a depth of 20mm (¾in). Measure 10mm (⅜in) from the top and bottom for the shoulders for the tenon.

Remove most of the waste with a hand drill and chisel the rest away until you reach the markings. Make sure all the debris at the bottom is properly cleared away. Use a ruler to verify the depth of the mortise.

Measure and mark out the width and depth for the tenons. Saw the waste and clean up with a chisel or shoulder plane. One method is to cut the tenons slightly oversized and trim them down with a shoulder plane or a chisel to fit into the mortise.

Check and fit the tenon into the mortise. If there are gaps, check that the shoulders are all straight and level. If the tenon does not go fully down, check the depth of the mortise or trim off the length of the tenon.

Measure the depth of the mortise and transfer the marking to the cross support for the length of the tenon. Divide the width of the cross support by three to get the thickness of the tenons. Measure 10mm (⅜in) on the short sides of the end grain of the cross brace to get the width of the tenons.

Comparing both joints, the placement of the tenon will affect the position of the cross support because of the offset made by the shoulder of the tenon. You can see the additional space needed when making a fully shouldered tenon.

HOUSING JOINTS

Housings are grooves which are cut across the grain and are normally used horizontally for shelves. They can also be used vertically to increase the structural stability between pieces of wood. However there is little mechanical strength on its own unless used with glue or fasteners such as screws. One way to make the housing joint stronger is to make it a dovetail housing which pulls both sides together mechanically. For this project a variation of a stopped dovetail housing joint is used.

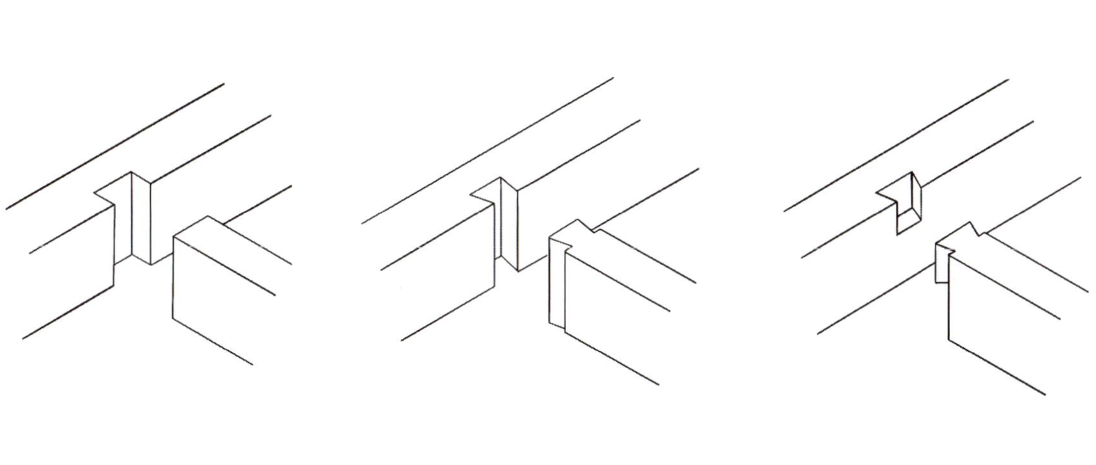

From left to right: a housing joint, a dovetail housing joint, a variation of stopped dovetail housing joint.

TORSION BOX-STYLE BENCH TOP 3 – MAKING A DOVETAIL HOUSING JOINT

Measure out the dovetail using a bevel gauge with the angle of roughly 15 degrees. Use a marking gauge to scribe the depth of the dovetail to establish the shoulder lines.

Cut away the waste and saw the shoulders of the dovetail. Clamp the workpiece down before trimming it down with a chisel.

Measure the centre point between the two cross supports, transfer the dovetail profile onto the sides with a marking knife and scribe the depth using a marking gauge.

Make multiple relief cuts with a saw to help remove the material efficiently. Then, use a chisel to gradually clear out the waste, ensuring the base is flat and the depth remains even and straight.

Fit the dovetail into place. If the joint is too tight, inspect all surfaces to ensure they are flat and levelled. If it is too loose, reinforce it by adding strips of veneers to build up the joint.

Assemble the joints to form the frame of your torsion box-style bench top. If required, apply glue to secure them, ensuring everything is square and aligned before the glue sets.

ATTACHING THE WORKTOP

For the worktop, you can choose a manufactured board like plywood or MDF or a solid piece of wood if you prefer. I decided to use jointed pine boards and to only cover three-quarters of the surface so that I can use one side as my clamping area.

The best thing about this method of construction is that you can always decide to change the top when you want to. You can attach the top by screwing it directly onto the frame, or use fasteners like threaded inserts for repeatability. However this method means that the screw head will be visible on the surface of the bench top.

One way of attaching tops without any visible screws on the top is to make 'buttons'. These are little blocks of wood that are screwed from under the top and have tabs that go into mortises on the base. They can be made in batches by cutting them off wider pieces of wood. The slightly elongated mortise allows for any wood movement on the tops.

The hollow area on the left side serves as a clamping solution as well as a mounting point for a small router table.

Buttons can be made in small batches by first making the step profile before splitting them into smaller units.

The elongated mortises allow for movement of the wood especially when using solid wood as the worktop.

REMOVING WASTE BETWEEN THE JOINTS

Traditionally, the removal of waste material between joints is done by the heavy striking of a mallet on a chisel, known as 'chopping'. This is a fast but also very loud operation. This continuous banging is not ideal for woodworking in an apartment. I generally avoid as much chopping as possible, or totally eliminate the use of this motion when possible. Four alternative ways of removing waste between joints without 'chopping' are shown below.

All of these steps end off with pairing and cleaning up with a chisel. The end grain between the joints has to be flushed or slightly undercut so that the joints will fit properly. Use a small square or a ruler to check if there is any debris or 'hills' to clear.

Use a fret saw or a coping saw to remove the waste as close to the shoulders as possible.

Make relief cuts, first vertically, followed by left and right diagonals to remove the bulk of material.

Drill holes close to the shoulder to make a perforation before knocking the waste out.

Make sloping cuts with a chisel towards the shoulder from both sides till they eventually meet and break off.

THE TRESTLE LEGS

Trestle legs are great as supports for a bench top and relatively easy to make. The height of the workbench should be measured to the height of the user. Therefore, after taking into account the thickness of the bench top, the length of the legs should be prepared accordingly. They can be left slightly oversized and sawn off later on.

The height of the workbench is very personal. Start with taller trestle legs so that you can modify them to suit your height later on.

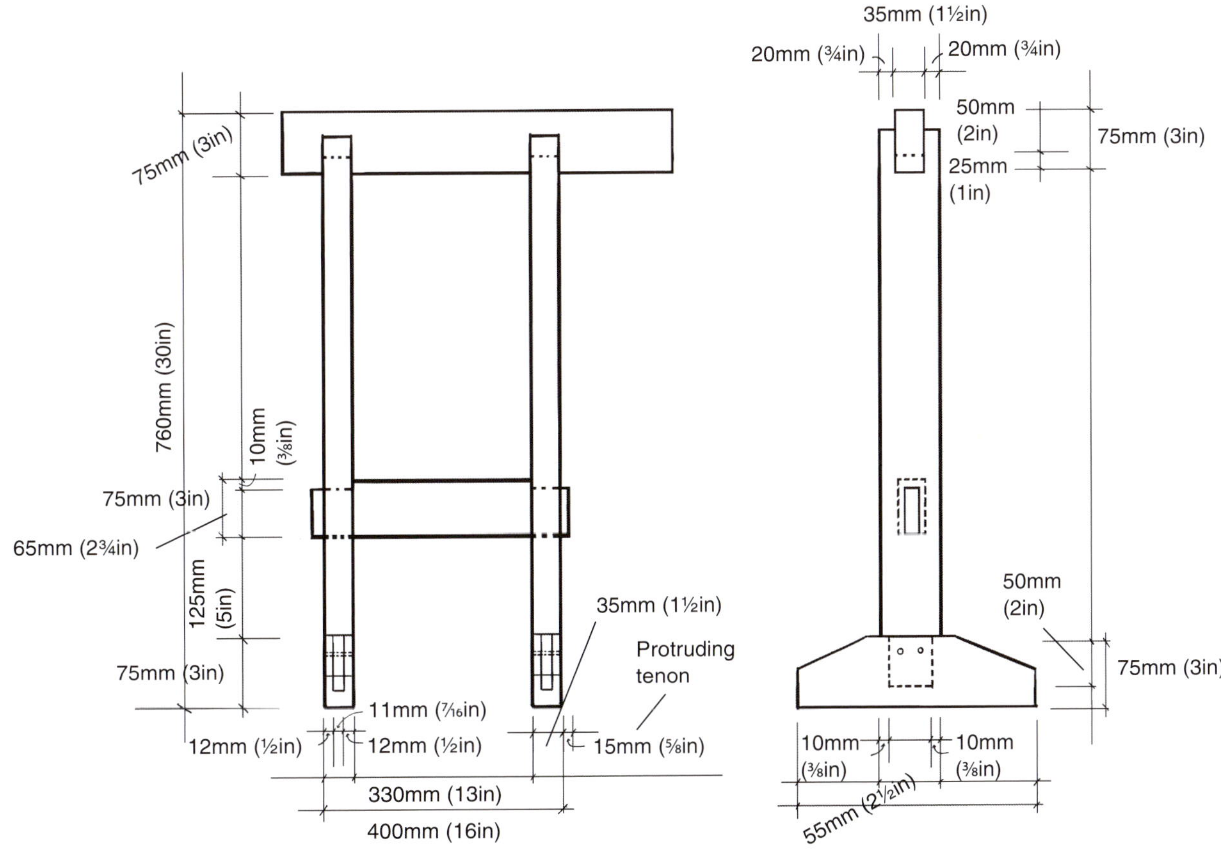

A trestle leg.

Cutting List for Trestle Legs (One Pair)

Part	No. of	Length	Width	Thickness	Material
Top Stretcher (with allowance for a tool well)	2	500mm (19¾in)	75mm (3in)	35mm (1⅜in)	Pine
Legs (allow extra if necessary)	4	700mm (27½in)	75mm (3in)	35mm (1⅜in)	Pine
Bottom Stretcher	2	330mm (13in)	75mm (3in)	35mm (1⅜in)	Pine
Feet	4	300mm (11¾in)	75mm (3in)	35mm (1⅜in)	Pine

MAKING THE TRESTLE LEGS

On the feet, find the centre point and measure out the width of the tenon. These are blind mortise and tenons and have 10mm (⅜in) shoulders on both ends, therefore the length of the mortise is (75mm - 10mm - 10mm = 55mm/2¼in).

The width of the mortise is typically one third the thickness of the stock being used. Therefore 35mm divided by 3 = approximately 12mm (½in). Use a marking gauge to scribe out the cheeks of the mortise. Mark out a line in the centre so it is easier to align the drill.

Remove the material for the mortise with a drill and clean up with a chisel. Use a smaller drill bit and pare to the knife marks. Make sure that the end wall of the mortise is as flat as possible and check that the depth of the mortise is relatively consistent throughout.

The depth of the mortise should be at least two thirds the height of the feet, to ensure that the tenon is deep and makes for a stronger joint. In this case since the feet are 75mm (3in) tall, the depth should be (75mm x ⅔ = 50mm/2in).

Cut the tenons. Start with cutting the cheeks before making the 10mm (⅜in) shoulders on both ends. Having shoulders helps with any rocking motion. I usually make my tenons with a slight taper so that I can shape them down later on to create a tight fit.

Dry-fit the feet. If they are too tight, trim the tenons. If they are too loose you can glue some wood veneer to thicken the tenons. You can create a profile to your liking at the ends of the feet or leave them as they are. They can also be drawbore-fitted later on (*see* 'Draw Boring' box later in this chapter).

To position where the lower stretchers should be, measure from the feet joints upwards so that both sides will be aligned with each other. The tenons on the stretchers will have one shoulder on the top. This makes the tenon sit exactly where the mortises are cut. In this case, the mortise length is 75mm - 10mm = 65mm/2⅝in.

The space between the legs is designed to match the width of the bench top. These are through tenons and will protrude out of the legs by about 15mm. Therefore the distance between the shoulders is the total width minus the thickness of both legs and both 15mm (9⁄16in) protrusions at each end. (330mm - 35mm - 35mm - 15mm -15mm = 230mm/9in)

Prepare the mortises and tenons and dry fit them together. Once this is done, you can prepare the upper stretcher. The upper stretcher is longer than the lower stretcher and extends further to the back. This is to accommodate for a tool well that will sit on the back later on.

Saw the legs to the required height. A halving joint will be used to attach the upper stretcher onto the legs. Place the upper stretcher on the top edge of the legs, mark out a third of the width and cut a recess to accommodate the thickness of the stretcher. Do the same recess on the stretchers and they should lock in place.

Dry-fit the trestle legs. All joints should not have any visible gaps. If the joints are too tight, trim the tenons. If the joints are too loose, use some thin shims to reduce the size of the mortises. The trestle legs can be glued-up at this stage or can be further strengthened by draw-boring the feet. (*See* drawboring section below.)

DRAWBORING

Normally pegs or dowels can be used to lock joints together by drilling holes through them and driving a dowel through (with or without glue). However for drawboring, the holes are offset by a small amount (just around a millimetre) so that when the dowels are knocked through, it pulls in the receiving joint, further forcing the joint tighter inwards.

Bamboo chopsticks can be used as a cheap and convenient alternative rather than making the dowels yourself.

A pencil sharpener can be used to create a little chamfer on the ends of the dowels so that they can be driven into the holes easier.

To mark out where the positions of the holes are, assemble the joint together and drill through the feet but stop just after touching the tenon. Remove the tenon and using the markings made by the drill, shift a little towards the shoulder and make this new slightly off-centre hole. Reassemble the joint, then with gentle but firm taps, force the dowel into place.

Trestle legs are great starting supports for worktops because they are compact and can easily be customised to suit the dimensions of your workbench. When not used for woodworking, trestle legs are also easily convertible into shelves or shoe racks.

Trestle legs can be easily repurposed into extra shelves or shoe racks.

THE TOOL WELL

Some woodworkers hate a tool well because it can become a magnet for offcuts and other items and eventually be clogged up with useless stuff. I personally like it because it is a convenient temporary area for me to place my tools and to free up the surface of my worktop.

The tool well designed for this workbench can be flipped over and be used as an extension of your worktop. If you feel that a tool well is unnecessary for you, you can always omit this step and trim off the extra length at the back of the trestle top stretcher.

The height of the tool well should be measured from the top edge of the top stretcher to the height of your worktop. The length of the tool well should be around the length of your worktop. The width of the tool well can be customised to your liking but do consider the sizes of your commonly used tools like your bench plane in its lying position.

The construction of this tool well is a long tray secured with finger joints (or comb joints) and a screwed base. The base can be joined boards or any type of manufactured board like plywood. It cannot be too thin, otherwise it may not be able to hold your heavier tools. I am using 15mm (⅝in) pine boards that I have joined together to make my required width.

Love it or hate it, a tool well can divide woodworkers.

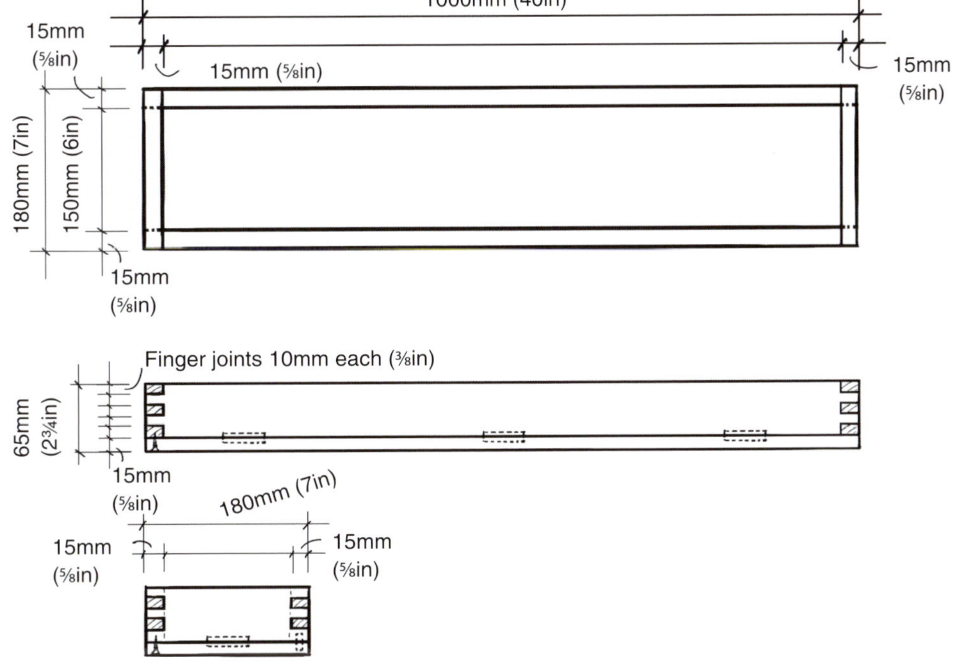

Illustration plan of a tool well.

Cutting List for a Tool Well

Part	No. of	Length	Width	Thickness	Material
Long sides	2	1,000mm (40in)	50mm (2in)	15mm (⅝in)	Pine
Short sides	2	180mm (7in)	50mm (2in)	15mm (⅝in)	Pine
Base	1	1,000mm (40in)	180mm (7in)	15mm (⅝in)	Pine

MAKING A TOOL WELL

Set your marking gauge to the thickness of the sides and scribe onto the face sides using the end grain as reference, marking the depth of the joint. Divide the width into five equal parts and mark them out. These will be called the fingers.

On the long sides, cut out the alternate fingers, see: Making a torsion style-bench top part 1 – (single finger joint). If the piece is too long to clamp up vertically, you can also saw it while laying it on the table.

Place the long side squared over the end of the short side and transfer the markings of the fingers. Scribe and cut away the unwanted parts. I usually cut a little short of the lines and trim to fit later on.

Fit all the joints together creating the carcass. Use a dab of glue to secure the joints. Measure the base over the tool well and attach it to the sides. I used loose tongues but you can also use countersunk screws to screw them in.

To prevent the tool well from being pushed over, you can screw a small piece of wood onto the back of the top stretcher or use dowels to hold it in place. Take note that you will be screwing into end grain and pilot holes are recommended.

ASSEMBLING THE WORKBENCH

To attach your worktop onto the legs, you can create a housing or make a false housing with two strips of wood screwed on the underside of the worktop. This helps to keep the worktop sitting in place and prevents it from shifting around too much. Follow the width of the top stretchers of the legs when you measure the width for the housing.

To further stabilise the workbench, a board of plywood can be cut to be placed on the trestle bottom stretchers. This will also become an additional shelving space.

A housing, the fitting of two strips of wood, or the combination of both can be created to fit the top leg stretcher onto the worktop.

The completed workbench presented by Stewie the cat to show the size ratio.

WORKBENCH UPGRADE

There are many ways to improve the stability of your workbench. You can consider installing a cross brace or stretchers between the legs to reduce the rocking movement. Another effective way is to build a cabinet and install it beneath the bench top. This not only adds weight and increases rigidity, but also provides much needed storage space.

The main carcass of the cabinet will be made with mitred dovetails, very similar to the dovetails in the toolbox project, but with a slight variation at the corners. Mitred dovetails are great to conceal any through-grooves for the purpose of installing a backing board. They also look more refined from the front and less 'chunky' as compared to the basic dovetail.

For this under-workbench-cabinet, I have designed it to have left and right compartments, with one side having drawers and the other as a larger open storage space. You can always configure your cabinet to your own design and requirements. This design will include instructions for basic drawer making as well as how to make a pair of sliding doors for the front.

Prepare your materials for the basic carcass. I measured the internal dimensions under my workbench and prepared some 15mm (⅝in) jointed pine boards. I decided to leave a small gap between the worktop and the cabinet as a shallow storage area or a possible drawer or tray in the future.

Making an under-workbench-cabinet not only increases storage space, it also helps with the stability of the workbench.

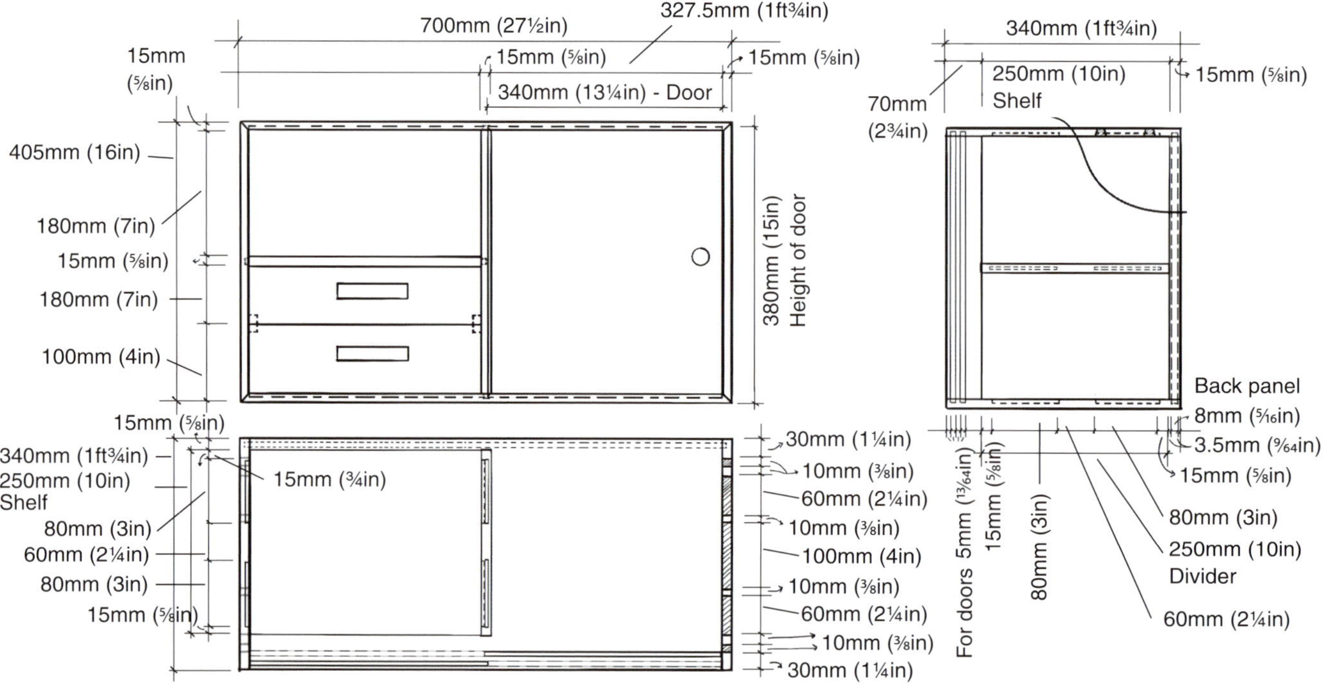

Illustration plan for a workbench cabinet.

Cutting List for Workbench Cabinet

Part	No. of	Length	Width	Thickness	Material
Sides	2	400mm (15½in)	340mm (13¼in)	15mm (⅝in)	Pine
Top and Bottom	2	700mm (27½in)	340mm (13¼in)	15mm (⅝in)	Pine
Centre Divider	1	390mm (15⅜in)	260mm (10¼in)	15mm (⅝in)	Pine
Left Shelf	1	335mm (13¼in)	260mm (10¼in)	15mm (⅝in)	Pine
Back Muntin	1	390mm (15⅜in)	60mm (2⅜in)	15mm (⅝in)	Pine
Back Panels	2	390mm (15⅜in)	315mm (12⅜in)	4mm (5⁄32in)	Pine
Front Sliding Doors	2	390mm (15⅜in)	340mm (13¼in)	4mm (5⁄32in)	Pine

MAKING A WORKBENCH CABINET

1

Measure and cut out the tails like a regular set of dovetails. The only difference is to leave a much wider space for the first half tail. Leave a space of 40mm (1⅝in) to account for two sliding doors which are 5mm (¼in) thick each. There will be two grooves at the front for the sliding doors and one at the back for the back panel.

2

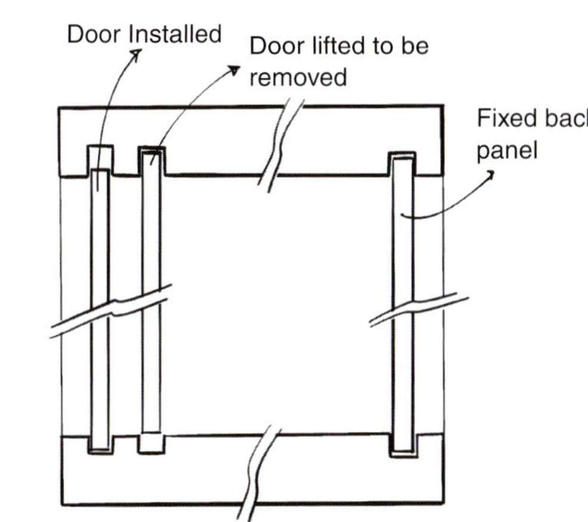

Measure 30mm (1⅛in) from the front edge and put a pencil mark. This is the area where the grooves of the sliding door will be made. Leave 5mm (¼in) spacings between the front and the back of the cabinet. The depths of the upper grooves are deeper by more than half of the lower ones to allow the doors to be removable.

3

Use a marking knife to scribe out the 45-degree angle on the top edge of the board. Cut at a 45-degree angle at the 30mm (1⅛in) mark. Remember not to cut through, but only on the internal surface as the mitre is hidden when both joints meet as the boards come together later on. (⅛)

4

Do the same with the matching boards with the pins except that now at the 30mm (1⅛in) mark, you have to cut through to accept the board with the tails. Cut most of the waste out and then finish off with either paring on a 45-degree ramp or just chisel slowly until you reach the correct angle.

At this point you can dry-fit the joint. Instead of using a mallet and knocking them in place, I used a pipe clamp that is long enough to slowly ease it into place. Cut grooves on all sides for the back panel and only the top and bottom for the front sliding doors.

If your cabinet is long, or if you do not want a continuous wide back panel, you can split the back into smaller sections by making vertical dividers known as muntins. This allows smaller boards to be used and also increases the overall stability of the structure.

For the centre divider, measure exactly half from the shoulder lines of the dovetails. This will be the exact centrepoint where your mortises should be made. My centre divider is a 15mm- (⅝in)-thick board, so I will make 5mm (¼in) mortises to accept 5mm (¼in) tenons.

Measure and divide one of the sides for a space for two drawers. I divided it equally into half but you can design and customise your own drawer sizes. The method of installation is the same as the centre divider using mortise and tenons. Dry-fit the components together.

Measure and cut the panels for the doors. They should overlap each other by less than the thickness of the centre divider. This is to allow full access to either side; especially the side with drawers that need enough clearance to be pulled out. The height of the doors should be the opening plus the upper grooves so that they can be fitted in. Drill holes as the door pulls.

DRAWER MAKING

There are countless ways to make drawers. This will differ depending on construction methods, choice of material and how 'traditional' you want to make them. Regardless of the sheer number of ways to make drawers, I feel that it is more important to understand how drawers function and why certain types of joinery are more suited for this purpose.

Dovetail joints were used for traditional drawer making because they provide a mechanical function when pulling the drawers outwards. Another version of the dovetail joint called a lapped dovetail or a half-blind dovetail is used more often for drawers as it hides the end grain of the tails on the drawer fronts. Different species of wood can also be used to accentuate the wood types; a classic example is walnut or oak drawer fronts with maple sides.

Drawer sides and the back are usually 6mm (¼in) or 8mm (5⁄16in) and made of quarter-sawn, straight-grained wood as they are more stable and less prone to any warping. Drawer bottoms are also usually straight grain and have their grain running from side to side to account for any seasonal changes. These days laminated plywood or MDF are commonly used as they do not have as many seasonal changes compared to a solid wood panel.

For this cabinet build, two drawers will be made for the lower half of the left side. The lower drawer is slightly taller than the upper drawer. I am using some quarter-sawn red cedar for the drawer sides.

I will show two ways of making drawers and how they differ from each other. The first method is a somewhat traditional method utilising drawer slips. Drawer slips increase the wearing surface and help with the longevity of the drawer. They were traditionally pinned to the drawer sides but these days, some wood glue will help keep them well in place.

For this cabinet, I will use the drawer runner as my drawer stops. This will ensure that my drawers do not hit the back of the cabinet and allows both the drawers to be flushed when in the closed position.

The overhangs on the drawers are deliberately designed this way to utilise the drawer runners as their drawer stops.

The first method (*left*) is a traditional way with drawer slips and dovetails for the back, whereas a simpler, second method (*right*) has the drawer bottom fitted directly into the drawer sides.

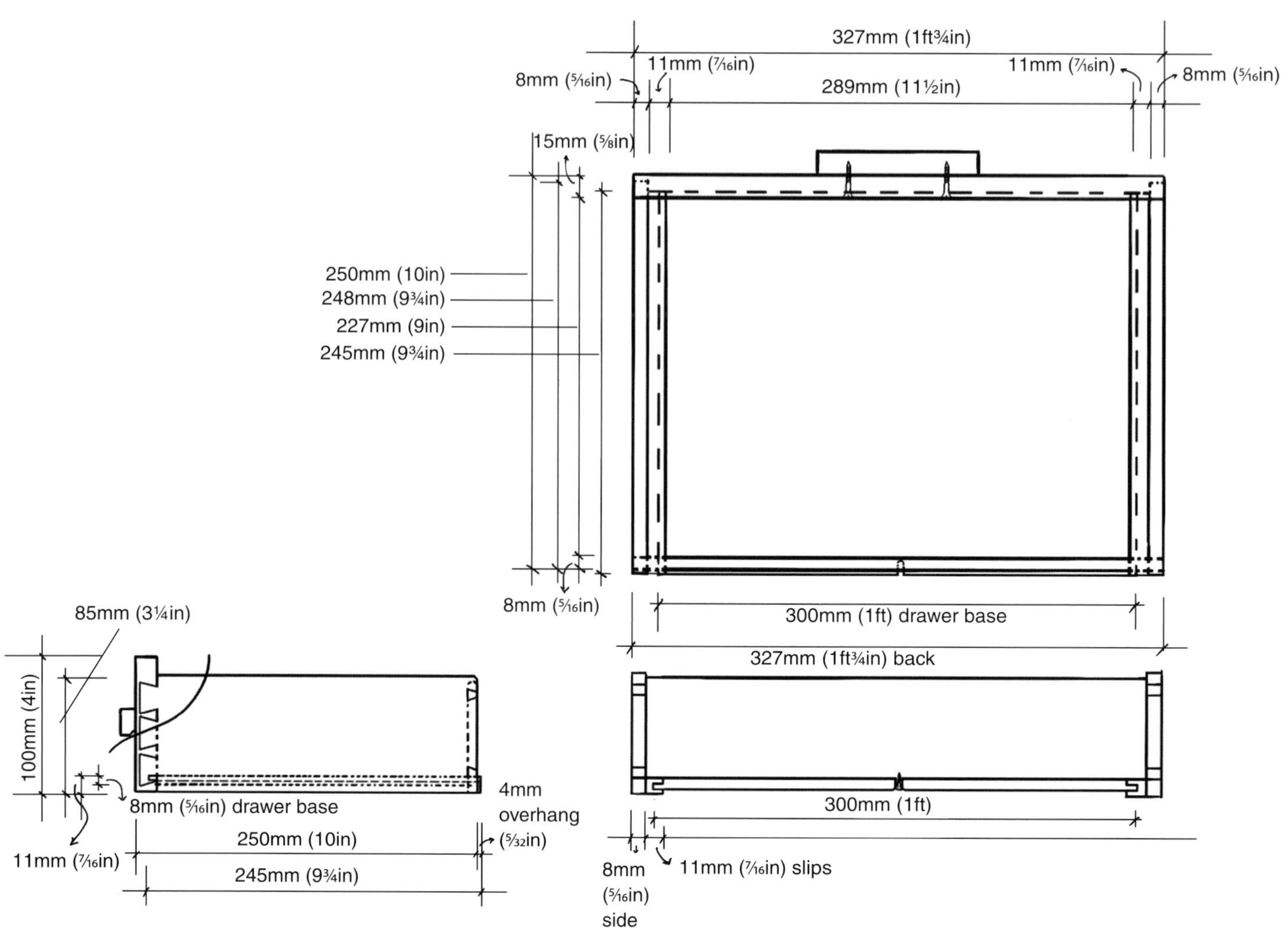

Illustration plan for a traditional drawer.

Cutting List for Traditional Drawer

Part	No. of	Length	Width	Thickness	Material
Front	1	330mm (13in)	100mm (4in)	15mm (⅝in)	Pine
Sides	2	250mm (9¾in)	85mm (3¼in)	8mm (5/16in)	Red Cedar
Back	1	330mm (13in)	70mm (2¾in)	8mm (5/16in)	Red Cedar
Base	1	245mm (9½in)	350mm (13¾in)	8mm (5/16in)	Pine
Slips	2	245mm (9½in)	11mm (7/16in)	11mm (7/16in)	Ash

MAKING A DOVETAILED DRAWER

Measure the opening for the drawer front, and the depth for the sides. The length of the front should have a very snug fit with a tiny allowance for some trimming later on. The back should be identical in length with the front. The sides, bottom and slips can be cut oversized for now.

Half-blind dovetails are cut almost the same as regular dovetails except that they are cut slightly shorter. This is when having two marking gauges will make things a little more convenient. One is set to the thickness of the drawer front and one is set to the length of the tails.

Cut the tails and transfer the markings to the drawer front. Take note of the placement of the drawer sides; they are flushed to the bottom of the drawer front as this is for the bottom drawer. You can put a small light underneath and use the light gap to aid in the positioning of when the shoulder lines meet.

Set a marking gauge to the thickness of the sides and scribe on where the joints meet. Transfer the markings of the pins downwards to this shoulder line. Remove the waste by first making diagonal cuts, followed by chiselling the depths before finally paring off with a chisel.

Cut grooves on the inner face of the front to accept the drawer bottom and the drawer slips. The groove should be just about the height of the drawer slips. The drawer slips have a groove to accept the bottom panel and are installed with a bare-faced tenon to the drawer front.

Measure the depth of the drawer to have a small clearance to the cabinet back. This ensures that the drawer is not constantly hitting the back of the cabinet. Cut the dovetails for the back. The height of the drawer back is shorter by one thickness of the slips. The dovetails at the back are regular through dovetails but without shoulders on their sides.

Assemble the sides, front and back. Dovetail drawers normally do not require any clamping because their joints should interlock with each other and provide a tight fit. At this point, you can glue the drawer slips to the inner face of the drawer sides.

Trim and fit the drawer bottom to the drawer. The bottom can be glued to the front groove and should override the back by about 5mm (¼in) to account for any seasonal movements. It is then secured to the drawer back by a slotted screw.

Fit the drawer into the opening. Trim the sides with a hand plane to slowly fit the drawer in. You can also over-trim the back half of the drawer more so that it slides in easily but has a gradual snug fit when fully pushed in.

AN ALTERNATIVE WAY OF MAKING A DRAWER

The second method is a simpler method whereby making grooves on the front and the sides for the base and joining the back with a full thickness housing into the sides. Measure the opening for the drawer front, back and the exact height and depth for the sides. This time, the dovetails should flush with the top of the drawer front, as this is for the top drawer.

Follow steps 1 to 4 for making a traditional drawer. Cut grooves on the sides for the drawer base and housing for the drawer back.

This simpler method of making drawers has grooves on the front and sides to accept the drawer base directly.

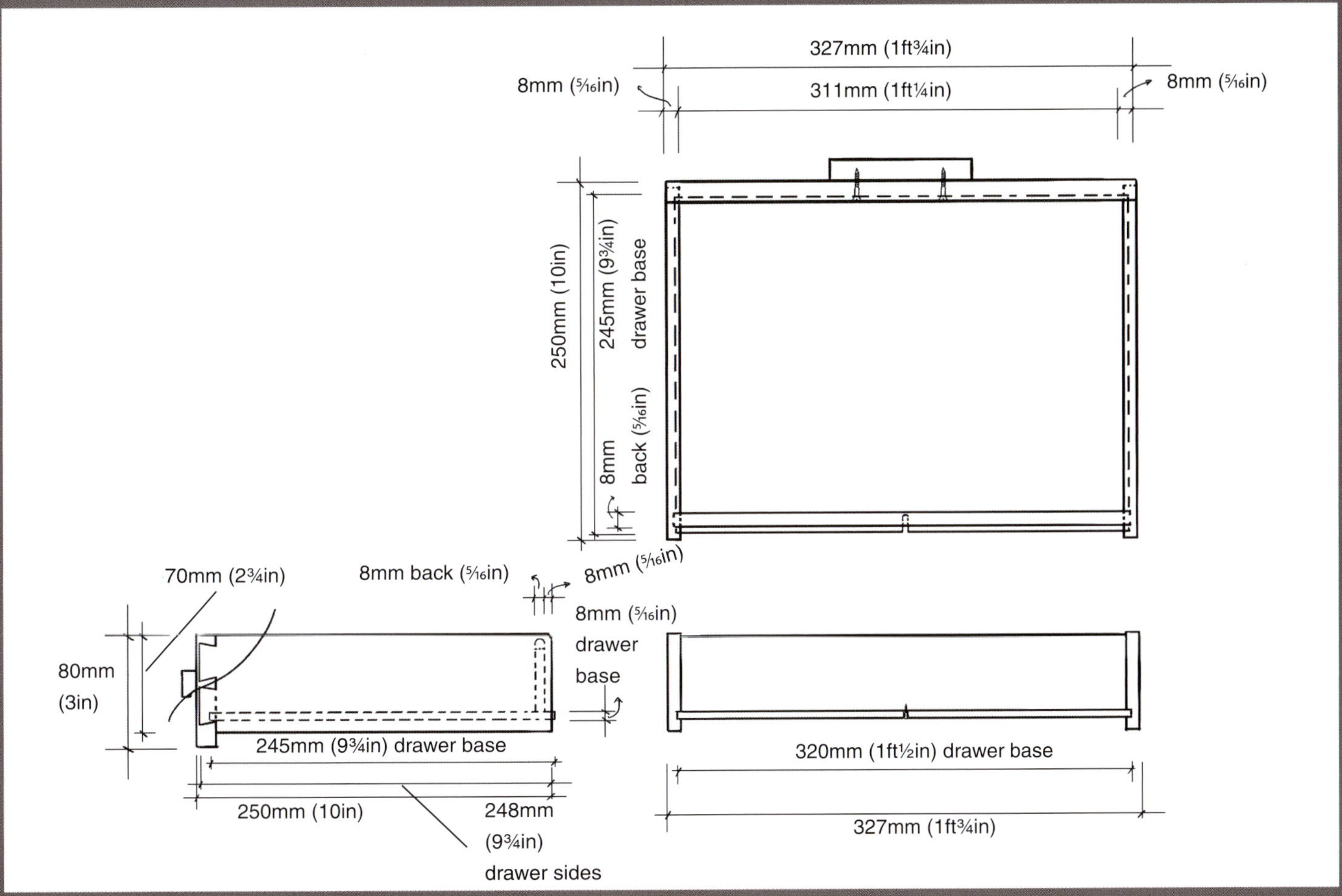

Illustration plan for a simplified drawer.

DRAWER RUNNERS

Drawer runners can be made with a slotted opening so that you can adjust their position later on.

Drawer runners can be installed by using the lower drawer as a spacer to guide you. This will also dictate the height of the upper drawer.

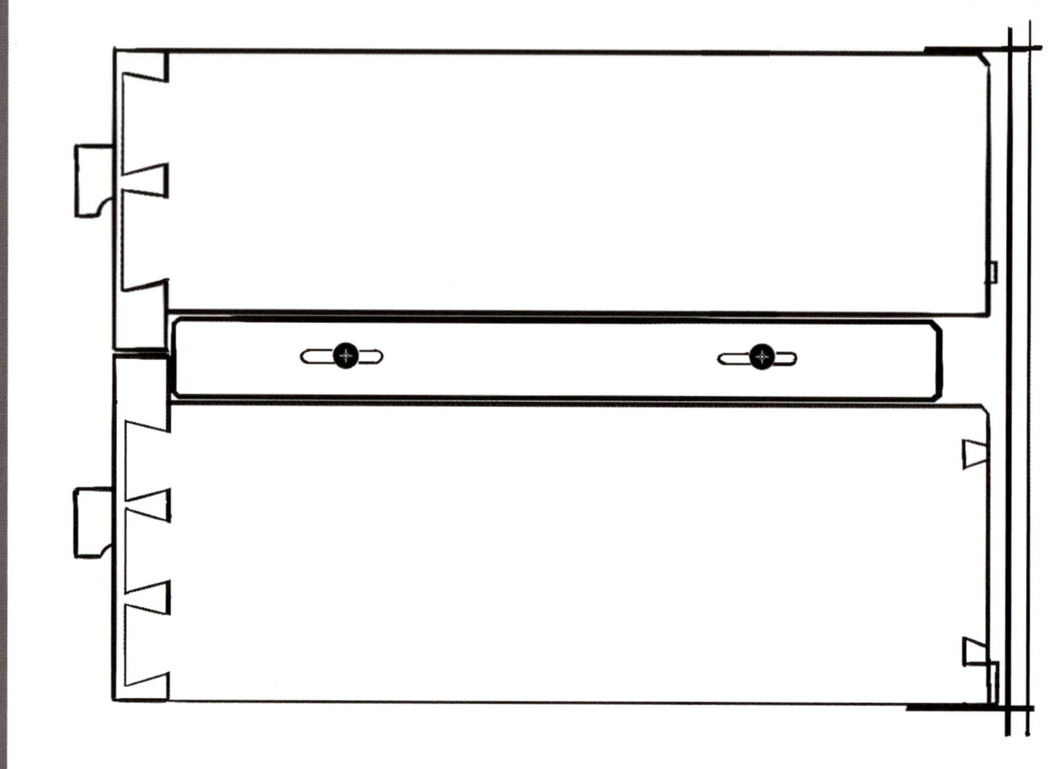

How the drawer runners also work as drawer stops when they make contact with the back of the drawer fronts.

FITTING THE DRAWERS

In both examples, you can glue the drawers up and leave them clamped overnight. Ideally, the interlocking joints will not need much clamping pressure and tapping them in place should be enough.

Once the glue is set, they can now be fitted into the cabinet. Do not make the mistake of pushing both drawers in without first putting some tape as a temporary drawer pull. If they are too tight, they might get stuck together and you might have some trouble trying to get them out. Use a block plane to gradually trim the sides of the drawer so that they will fit snuggly.

Drawer handles or pulls can be made easily with small pieces of wood. You can shape them to the style you like or you can also purchase some that you fancy. Most drawer handles can be screwed in from the back.

SUMMARY

This under-the-workbench cabinet is an excellent starting point for any cabinet-style projects that you can design for yourself. The combination of dividers, the number and size of drawers, and the type of doors can all be customised to suit your style and needs. Have fun experimenting by mixing different materials for your own designs.

Use some masking tape as temporary drawer pulls in case they get stuck. Slowly trim to fit the drawers into place.

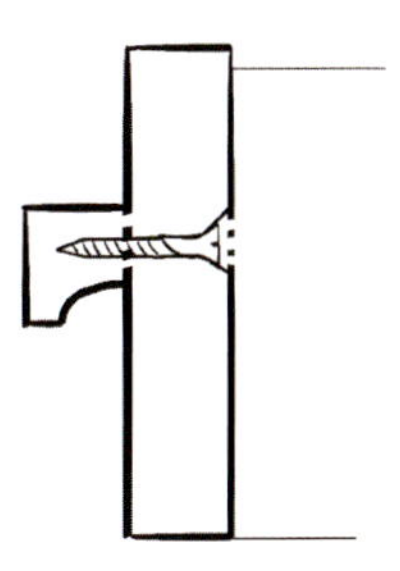

How to screw in a drawer pull from the back of the drawer front.

Drawer pulls can be made from offcuts and you can get creative and try out various shapes.

The exact same cabinet made for the workbench can also be used for your home items.

A few key products – glues, sandpaper and finishes can make all the difference to your project.

CHAPTER 9

ADHESIVES AND FINISHES

Projects are usually fun at the beginning – the selection of materials, choice of techniques and the making process can be both exciting and rewarding. However, when it comes to the later stages like gluing up and applying finishes, these are generally not met with the same degree of enthusiasm. The gluing up process can be messy and stressful, especially without proper planning and preparation. The arduous steps of filling gaps, sanding, applying polish and waiting for it to dry can feel tedious and somewhat disconcerting. Despite this, these steps are crucial to achieving a polished final project. In this chapter, I will introduce various adhesives, discuss surface preparation and guide you in selecting finishes for your project.

ADHESIVES

Organic

Animal, gelatine or hide glue, made from animal collagen (skin and bones) has been used since the time of ancient civilisations. It can be softened and reactivated with heat and moisture and is still used extensively in furniture and musical instrument making as well as antique restoration. It is typically sold in granules or in powder form and must be dissolved in warm water before application.

Synthetic

PVA (Polyvinyl acetate) adhesive, also known as 'white glue', is one of the most widely used adhesives for crafts and can

Adhesives made from organic sources like animal proteins as well as modern synthetics.

be found easily at stationery supply outlets. Woodworking PVA adhesives are modified to be more suitable for woodworking, because they offer additional attributes such as water resistance and added bond strength.

Common brands include 'Titebond', 'Gorilla' and 'Elmer's'. Most brands have different varieties, each tailored to specific needs. I generally use a faster-setting adhesive like Titebond II for general glue-ups and Titebond III for more complex, multi-step assemblies, due to its lower viscosity and longer open time.

Two-part epoxies are useful for bonding non-wood material onto wood. Depending on the type, they can set very quickly and are my go-to when I need to attach magnets or brass components into wood. Cyanoacrylate (CA) or 'superglue' can also be used for this purpose, but I personally avoid it due to its thin consistency and irritating fumes. Other resin adhesives such as urea-formaldehyde glue are used for specialised tasks such as boat building, veneering and lamination work.

Choosing the Right Adhesive

My main considerations when selecting an adhesive are its reversibility, open time, water resistance, and gap-filling properties. Some other considerations include whether the adhesive can be easily sanded or stained after drying. For general woodworking and beginner projects, I recommend a PVA wood adhesive such as Titebond II or a similar product you can find in your locality. Since wood PVA has a limited shelf life, it is best to buy only what you need to avoid waste.

Before any glue up, it is always important to go through the steps in your head and when possible to do a test run. Clamps can be set to their openings and the surface used for the adhesion process should be clear of any tools or material not needed. Clamping blocks or wedges should be within arm's length and cloths needed to clean up any spillage should be readily available.

Finding the right amount of glue for a successful glue-up is also crucial. I tend to dislike an excessive use of adhesive to a point where it drips everywhere and become a mess to clean up. My rule of thumb is to apply just enough so that when the parts are clamped together, a thin bead squeezes out along the joint. While some woodworkers will wait for the adhesive to partially dry before peeling it off, I prefer to wipe away any excess immediately with a damp cloth. Leaving ample drying time is also an important factor. I always try to leave my glue-ups overnight after clamps are put in place. The last thing you would want is your pieces to fall apart at this stage.

'GLUING UP'

In general, any product used to adhere two materials together is called an adhesive. The term 'gluing up' is often used in woodworking as a verb to describe the process of using adhesives in joinery. This was accurate in the past because, traditionally, most adhesives were made from animal sources, and these are referred to as animal glue.

However, modern adhesives are typically synthetic polymers rather than animal-based, so it is more accurate to refer to them simply as adhesives instead of glue. Modern synthetic adhesives will include things like Polyvinyl Acetate (PVA), epoxy and cyanoacrylate (CA).

A common misconception is calling all wood adhesives 'wood glue', when in fact different types serve specific purposes. Another mistake is assuming stronger adhesive equates to a stronger joint – joint design and clamping pressure are just as crucial.

SURFACE PREPARATION

Even if you do not intend to apply any finishing product, you might still want to clean up the surfaces of your project from any glue stains and pencil marks. Surface preparation also includes filling up any gaps or small voids prior to sanding.

Remove any glue stains with a scraper or gently with your chisel. Sanding hard directly on thick glue spots might actually 'smudge' it, making it harder to clean off. Pencil marks can also be removed at this stage.

Glue stains, pencil marks and gaps – surface preparation is an important step before applying any finishing product.

FILLING UP THE GAPS

Wood fillers can be used to fill small gaps or cracks. There are many available to purchase or you can simply make up your own. I like to use a mixture of fine sawdust and PVA glue. Over the years, I have collected sawdust from various species of wood to match the colour of different projects. Here is a simple way to make it.

Some fillers do not take stains very well and should be tested prior to applying them on your project. You could also make 'stained' fillers by adding some water-based colour dyes or pigments to the filler mix.

Water-based pigments can be added to the filler mix to create a colour to match your wood type.

MAKING A WOOD FILLER

The ingredients to make a simple water-based wood filler are wood dust, water, and PVA. I keep a selection of wood dust from different species for different-coloured wood fillers.

Collect sawdust during sawing or sanding operations. You can even get finer sawdust if you sift it through a fine mesh, which makes for better fillers.

Mix the sawdust with water in a 1:2 ratio. It should look like a wet sand mixture. If it is too wet and runny, add more sawdust; if it is too dry, add a dash of water.

Wrap the sawdust mixture in a piece of cotton cloth and squeeze all the water out. It should now look like a lump of kneadable dough.

Add some PVA or wood glue into the dough and mix it into a paste. Add a little glue each time to get a smooth and lump-free consistency.

Apply as needed. If the gaps are deep, apply a little at a time and repeat progressively. Once dried, sand off gently with 180 grit sandpaper.

SANDING

Sanding can be messy and dusty and is probably one of the main reasons most people would not want to do woodworking at home. However, it can be controlled and managed properly. If possible, be in a properly ventilated area or near a window with a fan blowing outwards. Otherwise, bring your sanding operation nearer to the ground so that the dust created from sanding can quickly accumulate on the floor rather than floating around in the air too much. This way you can sweep up or use a vacuum cleaner after each round of sanding.

Both silicon carbide and aluminium oxide sandpapers are commonly found and they yield similar results for woodworking. Generally, silicon carbide sandpapers wear down faster but are harder and sharper, while aluminium oxide sandpapers are more durable and can last longer. What is more important though is the understanding of the grit numbers. The grit number represents the number of abrasive particles per square inch of sandpaper. The higher grit-number means more, smaller particles, resulting in the finer and less aggressive sandpaper, while the lower grit-number means fewer but larger-sized particles, making the sandpaper rougher and more aggressive.

Left: 180 grit silicon carbide sandpaper; *Right*: 180 grit aluminium oxide sandpaper.

From left: 120 grit, 180 grit, 240 grit, 320 grit, 400 grit sandpaper.

How to sand properly

When using sandpaper for larger surfaces, I use a sanding block with a piece of cork attached to it. This makes the sanding block more forgiving as it navigates through uneven surfaces. When using a sanding block, tightly wrap a piece of sandpaper around the block.

For smaller areas or hard to reach corners, use smaller pieces of sandpaper folded into thirds. This helps the sandpaper to not slip around when using it.

Do sand along and with the grain and generally not across it.

Do use even pressure and long strokes.

Do follow each grit progressively and not skip grit 180 → 240 → 320

Do NOT concentrate on one area for too long.

Some woodworkers will include a step known as 'raising the grain between sanding grits'. Water is applied on the surface to allow the wood fibres to stand up, which will then be sanded away with the next grit of sandpaper. This creates a smoother surface and is usually done as the final step before the application of a finishing product. I usually use a spray bottle with alcohol instead as it evaporates faster, though some might argue that using alcohol does not raise the wood fibres as effectively as water.

Sandpaper Grit	Uses
# 80	For removal of old paint or very uneven surfaces.
# 120	Very coarse and used for initial sanding on very rough surfaces.
# 180	A good starting point for most woodworking projects for surface smoothness.
# 240	A good stopping point for most polishes.
# 320–400	For a smoother surface or French polishing to a high glossy shine.
# 600	Used between coats of polish to lightly remove any fine dust and slight imperfections.

You can make your own sandpaper blocks with plywood or some wood offcuts and cork sheets.

Tear sandpaper using a ruler and fold smaller pieces into thirds.

DUST-FREE SANDING

I use a sanding system made by Mirka called Abranet®. It uses abrasive pads and can be fitted to any vacuum cleaner so that the dust is directly sucked away. This is one aspect that I really like because I can see my sanding progress immediately and while keeping the air dust free. I still switch back to small pieces of sandpaper for harder-to-reach areas and smaller sections, but this is my preferred method of sanding, especially on larger surfaces.

The abrasive pads come in various grits and are pretty long-lasting.

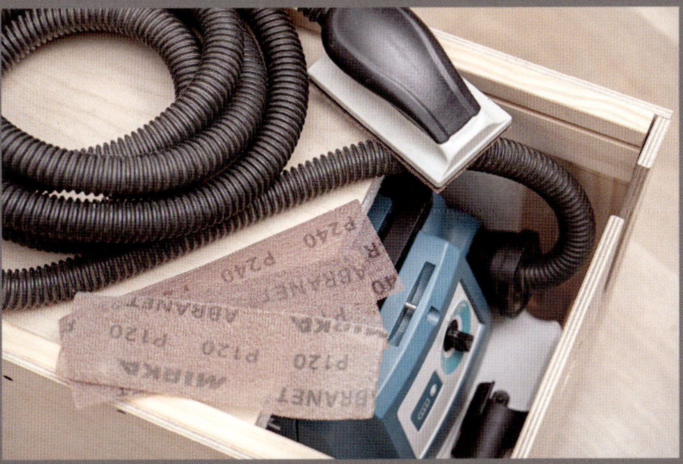

The vacuum sanding block is attached to a hose with an adaptor that can be fitted over your existing vacuum cleaner.

FINISHING

There are hundreds of finishing products available, making it easy to fall into decision fatigue when choosing a finish for your projects. Without going deep into the etymology of terms and their origins, I generally classify most finishes as a sort of coating on wood for the purpose of protection. Some finishes penetrate deeper into the wood, whilst some only remain as a thin layer on the surface. Some finishes also contain colour pigments or dyes, which can stain wood in a variety of shades.

Oils

Oils for woodworking finishes are mainly derived from seeds (tung oil, linseed oil, walnut oil). Some oils are mixed with petroleum-based thinners like mineral spirits to make them penetrate the wood better. Oils are mostly divided into drying (will polymerise and harden upon exposure to oxygen) or non-drying (remain liquid). Avoid non-drying oils like vegetable oil and olive oil on furniture because they will turn rancid. However if you are making cutting boards or kitchen utensils, you can use food-grade mineral oil, which does not turn rancid and is food safe.

Waxes

Natural waxes include beeswax made from the honeycomb of bees and carnauba wax made from the leaves of the carnauba tree. Petroleum-based waxes include paraffin and microcrystalline wax. Waxes offer minimal protection and have to be frequently reapplied. They are often also used as a topcoat with other finishes like shellac. You can also make your own wax polish with just a few ingredients (*see* box below).

From home-made waxes to commercially bought hard wax oils, the choice of wood finishes can be rather numerous and confusing.

Shellac

I treat shellac as a category of its own because it can be used to achieve a wide range of finishing styles. Shellac is made from the excretion of the female *Laccifer lacca* insect found on the branches and twigs it lives upon. Depending on the refinement of the crude 'stick-lac', colours of orange and red hues can be produced. The most refined, de-waxed shellac will result in a clear, almost transparent finish. This is the starting point of a tedious polishing technique known as 'French polishing,' which can result in a luxurious glossy finish often found in vintage furniture. Shellac can also be used as a type of sealer with other types of finishes. Shellac normally comes in flakes and is dissolved in alcohol before application.

Lacquers and Varnishes

These two terms have evolved over a long period of time, and their etymological meanings have been expanded through time. I have found it rather difficult to explain the distinct differences between modern varnishes and lacquers as they have many overlapping qualities and ingredients.

The word 'lacquer' could very well be derived from the above-mentioned shellac, from which the word 'lac' comes. The West also used this same term to describe an Asian lacquer '漆'(*qī*) or '*Urushi*' in Japanese, brought over to Europe in the sixteenth century. Traditional lacquer is made from the sap of the *Toxicodendron vernicifluum* tree. To replicate the same look without the same understanding of the actual processes and ingredients, European artisans developed their own recipes and concoctions of various oils and pigments to achieve a similar high-glossy look to this imported lacquerware. In modern days, the term 'lacquer' now comprises of synthetic resins like nitrocellulose or polyurethane dissolved in solvents that evaporate quickly.

Varnishes were traditionally made from natural resins like copal and dammar, dissolved in drying oils or solvents such as turpentine. They take a longer time to cure and are usually known to create a thicker, more protective film or coating on the surface. They are normally clear and transparent and may yellow over time. Modern varnishes, which include synthetic components, are divided into water-based or oil-based, and may include colour pigments and other additives.

In short, both modern varnishes and lacquers are some sort of protective or decorative coating made from some form of resin (natural or synthetic) and are dissolved and mixed with some type of solvent (water-based, oil-based, petroleum-based, etc). Lacquer dries faster through solvent evaporation while varnish cures more slowly through oxidation. Their durability, colour, glossiness and drying times vary among manufacturers and are sometimes very similar in chemical composition.

Hard Wax Oils

Hard wax oils are relatively new and they contain a mixture of waxes and oils. They are easy to use and can provide long-lasting protection on your wooden projects. Some of these products are non-toxic and have lower amounts of volatile organic compounds (VOCs), making them more suitable when used in a closed environment. I do still recommend using these products in a well-ventilated area. Some hard wax oils are also certified food safe and can be used on children's toys.

Choosing your finish

When I first began my woodworking journey, I started using shellac as my main finish as it had a decently long shelf life when it was in dry flakes. I only mix up a small amount of shellac polish whenever I work on a project. Shellac can be easily applied with a brush or a 'mop' and can be slowly layered to your desired look. I like applying about three or four layers and giving a little buff at the end to create a satin, semi-gloss look for my projects. As I progressed, I started using a combination of shellac and waxes, and then settled on using mostly hard wax oils as they were convenient and I liked the kind of finish they produced. I almost never use any spray product or products with high VOCs, like oil-based polyurethane.

For a start, I recommend looking for a product that is easy to apply, relatively quick-drying, and with low VOCs. Hard wax oils tick most of the boxes for working in an apartment and only a small amount of product goes a long way. My only complaint about hard wax oils is that they tend to dry up rather quickly after a tin is opened and form a layer of 'skin' above the product; which also means some form of wastage.

The Furniture Bible by Christophe Pourny is an excellent resource on the many types of finishes, stains and refinishing techniques.

Take care when using any chemicals, solvents and especially paint-stripping products. Do use proper masks, eye protection and gloves. I once had a little splatter of paint stripper that landed on an uncovered part of my arm and had a terrible burning sensation on that one spot for an entire day!

MAKING YOUR OWN WAX POLISH

The main ingredients of a wax polish are a wax and solvent. Beeswax, carnauba wax and paraffin can be used as the wax component. For the solvents, turpentine, food-grade oils like linseed oil and mineral oils can be used. Depending on what consistency and usage you are looking for, the ratios of each ingredient change. To store them, I use 30ml metal tins and sometimes recycled tins previously used for face creams and moisturisers.

A very basic beeswax furniture polish is a mixture of beeswax and turpentine. I like a 2:3 wax to solvent ratio but you can always adjust the ratios to your liking. The general rule is that the less solvent used, the harder the wax will become. However, different solvents might react differently, so you will have to experiment to achieve your ideal consistency.

Do use turpentine oil that is directly distilled from the resin of pine trees that smells of fresh pine leaves. A cheaper alternative that is also called turpentine is a by-product of the kraft paper manufacturing process and it smells rather foul and can cause irritation to the eyes and nose. Stay away from this, as it has a higher concentration of potentially harmful compounds. If you are unable to obtain turpentine oil, mineral oil can also be used.

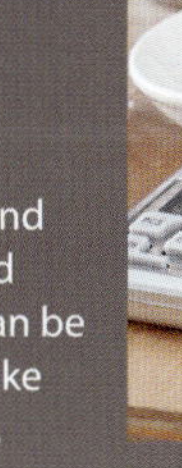

Both bleached and unbleached beeswax can be used to make wax polish.

MAKING YOUR OWN WAX POLISH

Basic wax recipe (This makes enough wax for a 30ml tin.)
20g Beeswax
30gTurpentine

If your beeswax comes in a block, grate it or cut it into smaller bits so that they will melt more easily. Put them into a heatproof jug set over a pot of simmering water like a double boiler. I use an electric cooker pot with a stainless steel trivet to raise the inner jug.

After the wax has melted completely, remove from heat and slowly stir in the turpentine. Make sure to mix it thoroughly. If the mixture begins to cool and solidify too quickly, put the jug back in hot water for a bit longer to fully incorporate the ingredients.

Pour the mixture into a glass or metal container to set. Metal tins or glass jars are suitable and work best. Plastic containers may not be suitable as the turpentine may react with the material, causing it to warp or 'melt'.

Leave the mixture to cool completely until it solidifies. Be sure to keep a record of the recipe and ratios so that you may tweak and experiment with different combinations and ingredients for future batches.

APPLYING YOUR WAX POLISH

There are some alternatives and recipes you can try and these include:

- Adding a few drops of lemon (or any of your preferred scent) essential oil for some fragrance just after adding the solvent.
- Adding oils to make it more creamy. Use food-grade oils if you will be using the wax on food utensils like wooden bowls or childrens' toys.

Use a soft scour pad to rub the wax polish onto the surface. Apply with gentle and even pressure to 'push' the wax into the grain of the wood.

The more you burnish the surface, the shinier it will become. It will gradually develop into a subtle sheen rather than a high-gloss finish.

To apply wax onto your projects, use a soft scour pad and rub some wax onto the surface. Once it is completely covered with wax, wipe off and burnish with a clean cotton cloth. The result is a simple, warm semi-shiny surface that shows off the grain of the wood.

The downside of a wax polish is that it sits on the surface and does not penetrate deep into the wood like oils. It does not offer much protection from water and will easily be the victim of the dreaded cup rings. However, it is still often used as a basic finish and it is easy to repair and re-apply.

SUMMARY

After all the time and effort invested in making your projects, the selection and application of a finish will truly make them shine. Understanding the different types of finishes will help you in choosing the right option for your work. This knowledge will also come in handy when you need to refurbish or refinish a pre-loved piece of furniture or when working with reclaimed materials.

Water rings can be easily removed by lightly going over the area with a soft scour pad and a small amount of wax.

Poupon the cat introducing the projects in this chapter – a chequerboard, a tray, a stationery box and a mitred keepsake box.

CHAPTER 10

PROJECTS

If you have followed this book from the beginning up to this point, you have most likely created quite a few things for yourself and I hope you are proud of what you have accomplished! Crafting meaningful projects is always a joy and completing each one brings a sense of satisfaction.

In this chapter, I will introduce some of my favourite beginner/apartment-friendly projects and guide you through the process of making them. These projects have been specially selected as they consist of essential woodworking techniques, which will help you build a strong foundation for your future designs. If you have attempted and completed the projects in the previous chapters, you should already have a good understanding of how to bring woodworking ideas to life.

PROJECT 1: VENEERED CHEQUERBOARD

This first project will show you how to work with wood veneers, cut them, and join them into a chequerboard pattern. This is one of the most basic patterns that can be used as a base or decoration for other projects such as boxes or drawers.

You will need some wood veneers (*see* Chapter 2, wood veneers) which can be purchased at craft stores or online suppliers. The basic tools you need are a ruler, scalpel or utility knife, a cutting mat and a straight piece of wood to use as a guide. When cutting veneers, use multiple light strokes with the tip of the blade. Applying too much force can break the fibres of the veneer, causing tears, instead of clean cuts. Depending on the type of blade, some woodworkers angle their blade slightly to ensure a 90-degree edge, allowing you to join veneers without gaps, much like how you would edge-join solid boards of wood to form wider panels.

I will be showing you how to create a simple chequered pattern using only one type of veneer. For more contrast, you can use two types of veneer to achieve a classic chessboard pattern. In this example, I am working with veneer sheets of approximately A5 size (148 × 210mm or 5 × 8in).

The chequerboard pattern is not just used for playing chess! It can be used as a decorative base for boxes or trays.

A chequerboard is a great start to exploring veneers.

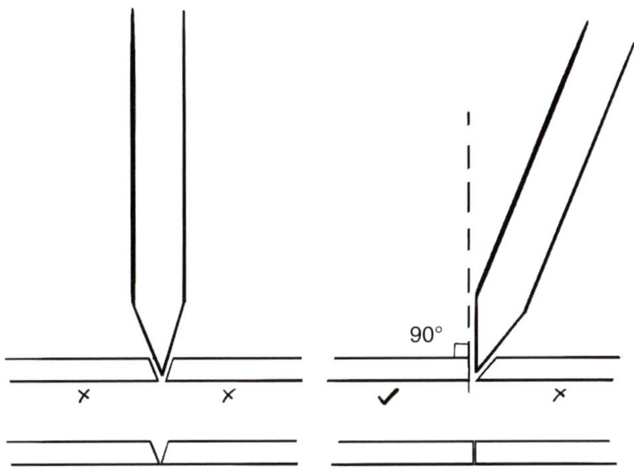

Showing the correct way of holding a blade to make a 90-degree cut.

Cutting List for a Veneered Chequerboard

Part	No. of	Length	Width	Thickness	Material
Chequerboard pattern top	3–4	210mm (8¼in)	148mm (6in)	0.6mm (1⁄32in)	Natural wood veneer (Mahogany)
Substrate	1	200mm (8in)	200mm (8in)	15mm (5⁄8in)	Birch Plywood
Lippings (optional)	4	210mm (8¼in)	18mm (¾in)	4mm (5⁄32in)	Teak
Veneered bottom	Your design	-	-	-	Natural wood veneer
Pressing boards	2	220mm (8¾in)	220mm (8¾in)	12mm (½in)	Plywood

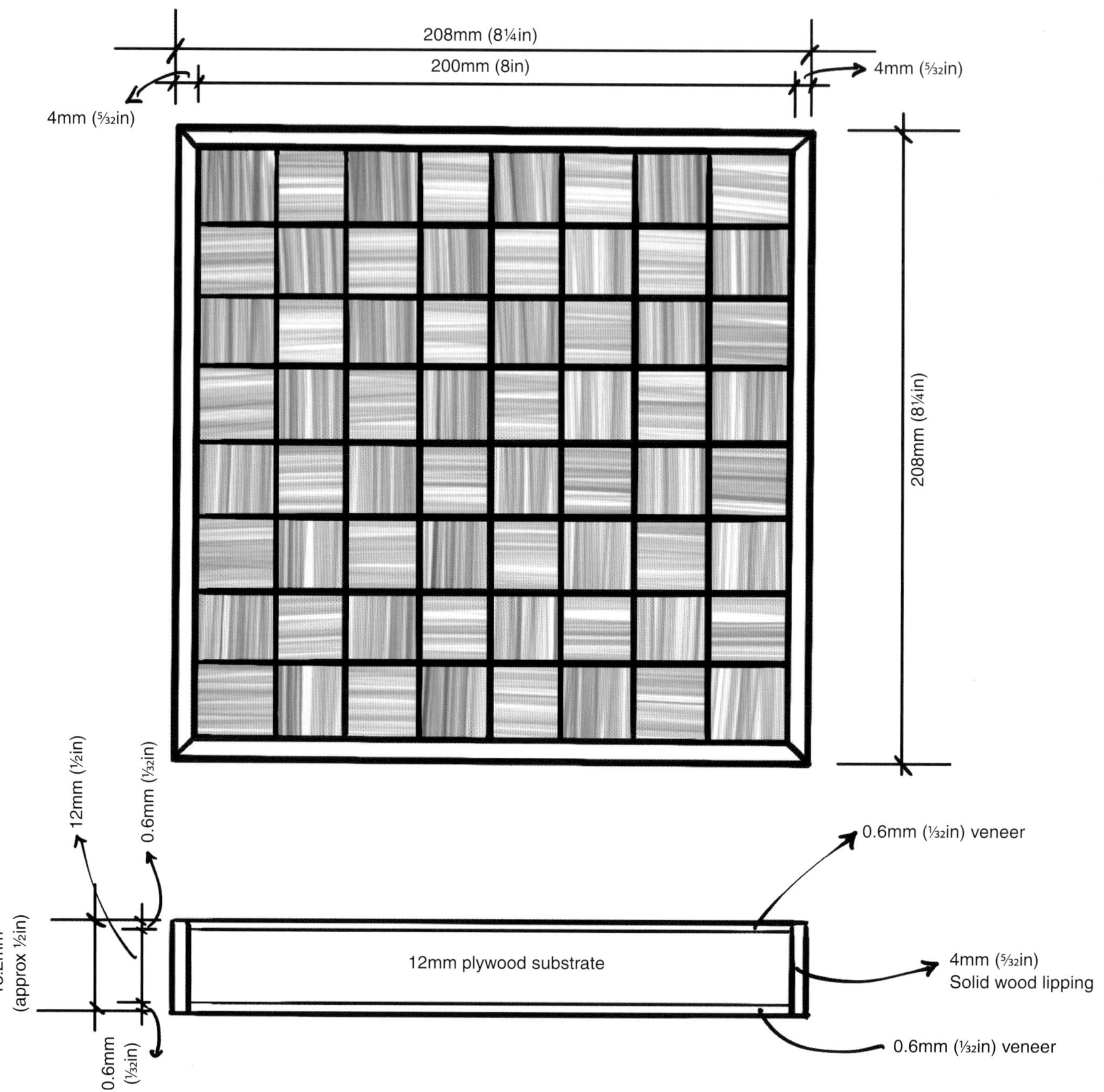

Illustration plan of a chequerboard.

MAKING A VENEERED CHEQUERBOARD

On a cutting mat, prepare the surface by clamping a straight piece of wood (or plywood) to the side of the table over the cutting mat. This serves as a guide for the veneer when cutting strips later on.

Prepare the veneer sheets by trimming approximately 5mm (¼in) from the edges to create a clean, straight reference side to work off. I also use chalk to mark one face of the veneer so that I can keep track of working off the same face throughout the process.

Push the reference side of the veneer against the guide, position your ruler over it and cut a strip. The width of the ruler will determine the width of each strip of veneer. Repeat the process until you have approximately six strips.

The same steps apply when cutting the veneer sheets in the other orientation. Cutting veneers across the grain can be a little challenging as they have a tendency to split. To minimise breakout, apply masking tape at the edges.

Once you have enough strips, arrange them in an alternating manner and use masking tape as a backing to hold them in place. I recommend joining them in pairs before gradually assembling them together.

To join the two pieces together, apply glue between each veneer pair either with your finger or a paint roller. Close the seam up and tape the other side. Gently 'stretch' the tape and use its elasticity to pull the veneers together gently.

Repeat step 6 to join all the pairs together into one large sheet. Trim off its side, making sure it is squared to the long edge. You can use the guides on the cutting mat or a square paired with a ruler along the edge of the cutting mat as the reference.

Push the trimmed side against the guide and continue to make strips as per step 3. When cutting through alternating grain directions, take extra caution and adjust your cutting force to prevent tear-outs or uneven cuts.

Tape and join into pairs as shown in step 6 — first in pairs then progressively forming them into a larger sheet. To ensure the sheet remains flat while the glue dries, keep the joined sheet under a board to weigh it down.

Trim off the excess parts and slowly remove all the masking tape. Be extra careful when removing the tape and always peel it off gently to avoid any fibre tear outs. The chequerboard sheet is now ready to be adhered onto a suitable substrate.

Prepare two pressing boards that are larger than your workpiece. Line them with waste paper to prevent your veneer sheet from getting stuck to the pressing boards. Have everything ready before you start the glueing-up process.

Apply glue onto the substrate with a paint roller and place your chequerboard sheet over it. Adjust its placement so that the veneer sheet is in alignment with the substrate. Tape the corners with masking tape to keep it from slipping.

Use as many clamps as possible, making sure that you apply even pressure throughout. An alternative is to have heavy weights over the pressing boards. Allow ample time for it to dry completely.

Once ready, remove from the pressing boards. Carefully clean off any glue residue by using a scraper or sandpaper, working slowly to prevent any accidental damage to the surface of the veneer. Always veneer both sides of your substrate to balance the board.

You can complete the sides by attaching a lipping to hide the substrate. Use thin strips of wood slightly wider than the thickness of the board, glue them directly to the edges of the veneered board and trim off the excess later.

The chequerboard or chessboard design is one of the most basic patterns that can be used as a base or decoration for other projects such as boxes or drawers. Experiment and combine this with other shapes to create other interesting patterns for yourself.

The completed chequerboard.

You do not need very large pieces of veneers to make decorative boards.

PARQUETRY

Popularised during the reign of King Louis XIV, 'Louis Cubes' are made with three different species of wood or a single species in varying grain directions to create a three-dimensional effect on an otherwise flat surface.

Parquetry is a form of decorative woodworking which is the piecing of wood together to form geometric shapes and patterns. The chevron and herringbone patterns are common parquetry designs used extensively for flooring. Louis Cubes – as shown in the accompanying image – are a great introduction to parquetry in decorative veneering.

Prepare strips of veneers and join them together lengthwise with tape. Cut a 60-degree angle using an isometric triangle ruler, commonly found in geometry sets.

2

Push this angled edge towards the guide and cut strips, using the same ruler you used when you created the individual strips.

3

Mix and match the individual parts to form your Louis Cubes. You can play with the different orientation of the grain direction of each veneer to form interesting effects.

PROJECT 2 : TRAY WITH CURVED HANDLES

This is a project that shows you how to manipulate wood to make simple curves. One of the common methods to make curved forms is to make a former that takes the shape that you want and a receiving one that sandwiches the material in between with the use of glue and pressure. However, to make these formers requires quite a bit of space, material and also machinery. As usual, I like to look at what I have in my home that I could use to achieve the same result. I found that round cake tins or moulds can make exactly what I need!

To make the curved tray handles you will need wood veneers or thin strips of wood around 1mm (1⁄32in) thick. For the tray base, a suitable board of wood that is wide enough and can accommodate the diameter of the cake tin.

A tray with curved veneered handles.

Curved profiles are normally made with formers, which are often large and chunky.

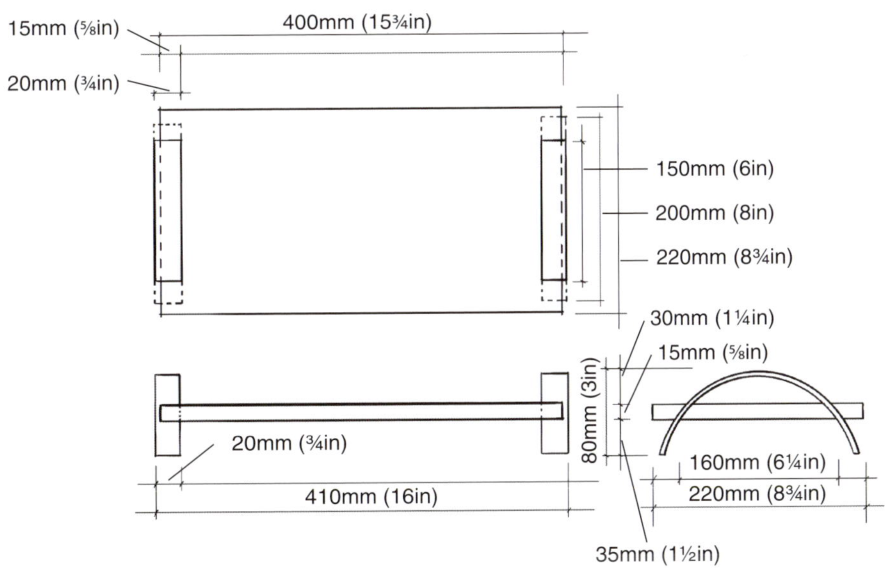

Illustration plan of a Tray with Veneered Handles.

Cutting List for a Tray with Curved Handles

Part	No. of	Length	Width	Thickness	Material
Base	1	400mm (15½in)	220mm (8¾in)	15mm (5⁄8in)	Camphor
Laminated handles (1 pair)	5-6 strips	320mm (12½in)	50mm (2in)	0.6mm (1⁄32in)	Natural wood veneer (Pearwood)

MAKING A TRAY WITH CURVED HANDLES

Prepare and cut the veneers into strips of around 25mm (1in) wide. Depending on the thickness of your veneers or wood strips, you will need a combined thickness of approximately 3–5mm (⅛–¼in) to achieve a stable handle. In this example, five sheets of 0.6mm (1⁄32in) veneers are used to make up 3.5mm (⅛in) thickness.

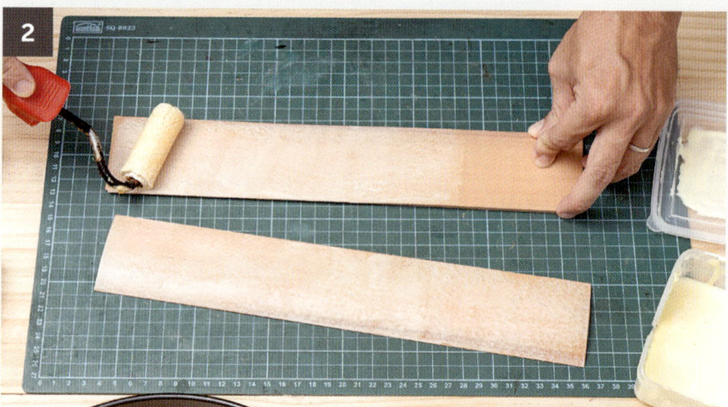

Apply PVA onto the veneers and stack them together. Place the stack along the inner side of the cake tin. Prepare some strips of plastic repurposed from document folders to form a barrier between the cake tin and the stack of veneers.

Use as many clamps as possible to apply pressure on the veneer stack towards the cake tin. Leave it to dry completely. Once dry, remove the clamps and clean up any glue residue off the sides and surfaces.

Depending on the depth of your cake tin, you either make two narrow handles separately, or one wide handle which can be split into two. To split the wide handle into two, use a marking gauge to scribe a line in the middle and saw it in half, making sure that their widths are identical.

Place the handles on the end of the tray base and determine how high the outermost point of the curve should be. You can use a block of wood as a spacer so that the heights of both sides will be the same.

Mark-out and cut slots into the tray base about two thirds the width of the tray handles. As the handles are curved, start by sawing a straight line down before shaping the rest with a chisel.

Fit the handles into the slot and mark out the remaining distance for a halving joint (*see* Chapter Eight – Making trestle legs). This is done so that the handles can sit more securely to the base and will prevent them from sliding off the base.

Use a marking gauge to mark out the depth of the joint. Remove the material using a fret saw and clean up with a chisel. Chiselling on joined veneers will feel slightly different, as there are layers of dried PVA in between.

Apply a small amount of PVA and fit the handles in. Next, flip the tray upside down and use a block of wood as a spacer to mark out the height of the legs. Carefully saw all the legs to the same height.

Clamp a sheet of 180 grit sandpaper onto the worktop and run the bottoms of the feet over to get them levelled and smooth. Round off any sharp edges and apply an oil or wax finish to complete your tray.

This elegant and sleek tray can also be a laptop or tablet stand to complement your workspace.

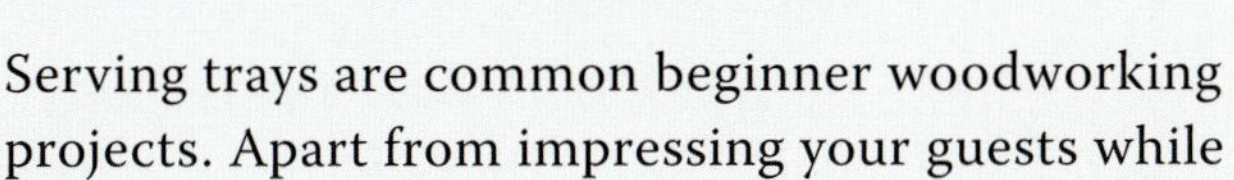
Serving trays are common beginner woodworking projects. Apart from impressing your guests while serving snacks, they can also be used as laptop or tablet stands.

PROJECT 3 : A STATIONERY BOX WITH SLIDING LID

This simple box is the ideal place to store your stationery or other personal items. The lid slides into place through grooves on its sides, thus no additional hardware is needed. The way it is constructed is similar to the trays for the toolbox (*see* Chapter Seven – Tray making), except for a few minor changes.

Measure and cut your material to size. It is easier to keep them in longer pieces when making the grooves before sawing them into their various parts.

I am using ash wood for the box construction, and cypress as my lid and base. Note that the front piece will be shortened after sawing off the top bit for the lid handle. I usually glue a strip of wood to extend its height.

The design of this box is simple, versatile, and does not require any additional hardware to attach the lid.

Each piece of wood consists of one long side and one short side.

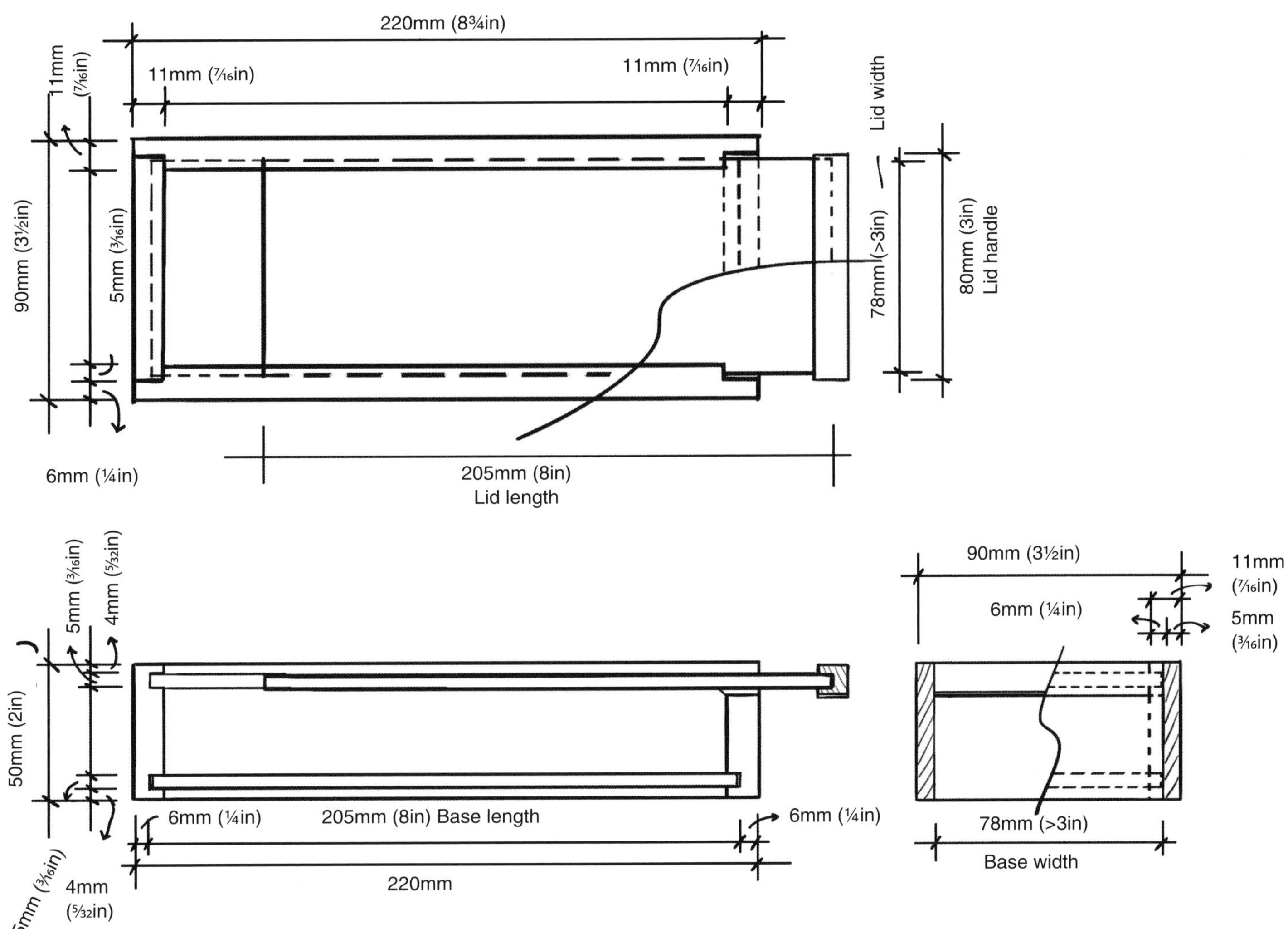

Illustration plan for a Stationery Box with Sliding Lid.

Cutting List for A Stationery Box with Sliding Lid

Part	No. of	Length	Width	Thickness	Material
Long sides	2	220mm (8¾in)	50mm (2in)	11mm (7⁄16in)	Ash
Short sides	2	80mm (3⅛in)	50mm (2in)	11mm (7⁄16in)	Ash
Lid	1	210mm (8¼in)	80mm (3⅛in)	5mm (3⁄16in)	Cypress
Base	1	210mm (8¼in)	80mm (3⅛in)	5mm (3⁄16in)	Cypress

MAKING A STATIONERY BOX WITH SLIDING LID

1

Prepare your timber and cut grooves for both the bottom and the lid. Both the lid and base are 5mm (3⁄16in) so the same tool can be used for both grooves. Make rebates on the longer sides to accept the front and back.

2

On the front piece, saw off a 10mm (3⁄8in) piece off the top for the lid. This piece will become the lid handle. You can use a different-coloured wood to extend the bottom of the handle as a visual cue for its upright orientation.

3

Dimension the base to size. The inner surfaces should be sanded and finished at this point. Plane the top edge of the front panel so that it sits lower than the grooves on the sides. Slope the grooves towards the front edge so that the lid can slide in easier.

4

Apply PVA and assemble the components of the box. Adhere the front handle to the lid. Masking tape and rubber bands can be used as an alternative to hold the workpiece in place during glueing-up, but clamps will provide better pressure.

5

Trim the length and width of the lid so that the handle sits in the groove when in the closed position. Apply wax into the grooves and the sides of the lid for it to slide in and out nicely. Your stationery box is now complete.

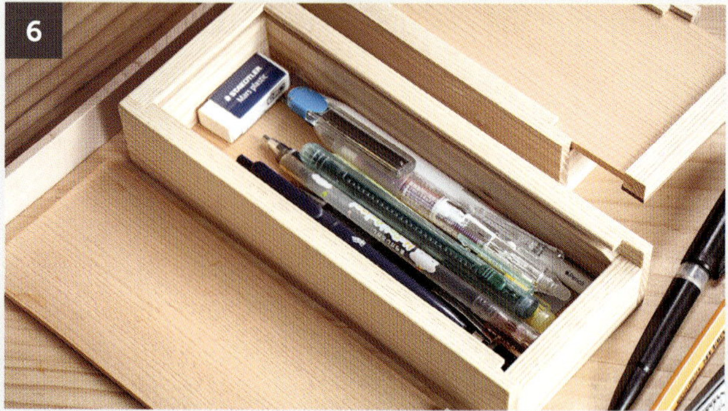
6

Apart from stationery, this style of sliding box can easily be modified in size to contain any other items.

PROJECT 4 : A MITRED KEEPSAKE BOX

Boxes remain one of my favourite things to design and build. Their construction follows the same principles as other forms of furniture making. A wall cabinet is essentially a tall box on its side, while a table can be seen as an inverted box without walls.

The most basic type of box is made up of a number of sides, a base and a lid. There are countless ways to connect these parts together. As you learn more types of joinery, you will also discover new ways to connect pieces of wood together. This is the same with how you attach the base and the lid to the sides. The different methods will alter the aesthetic of the box, so pick and choose what you like.

A beautiful, timeless keepsake box.

Matching up the grain will give a nice flow around the box, especially when using mitres.

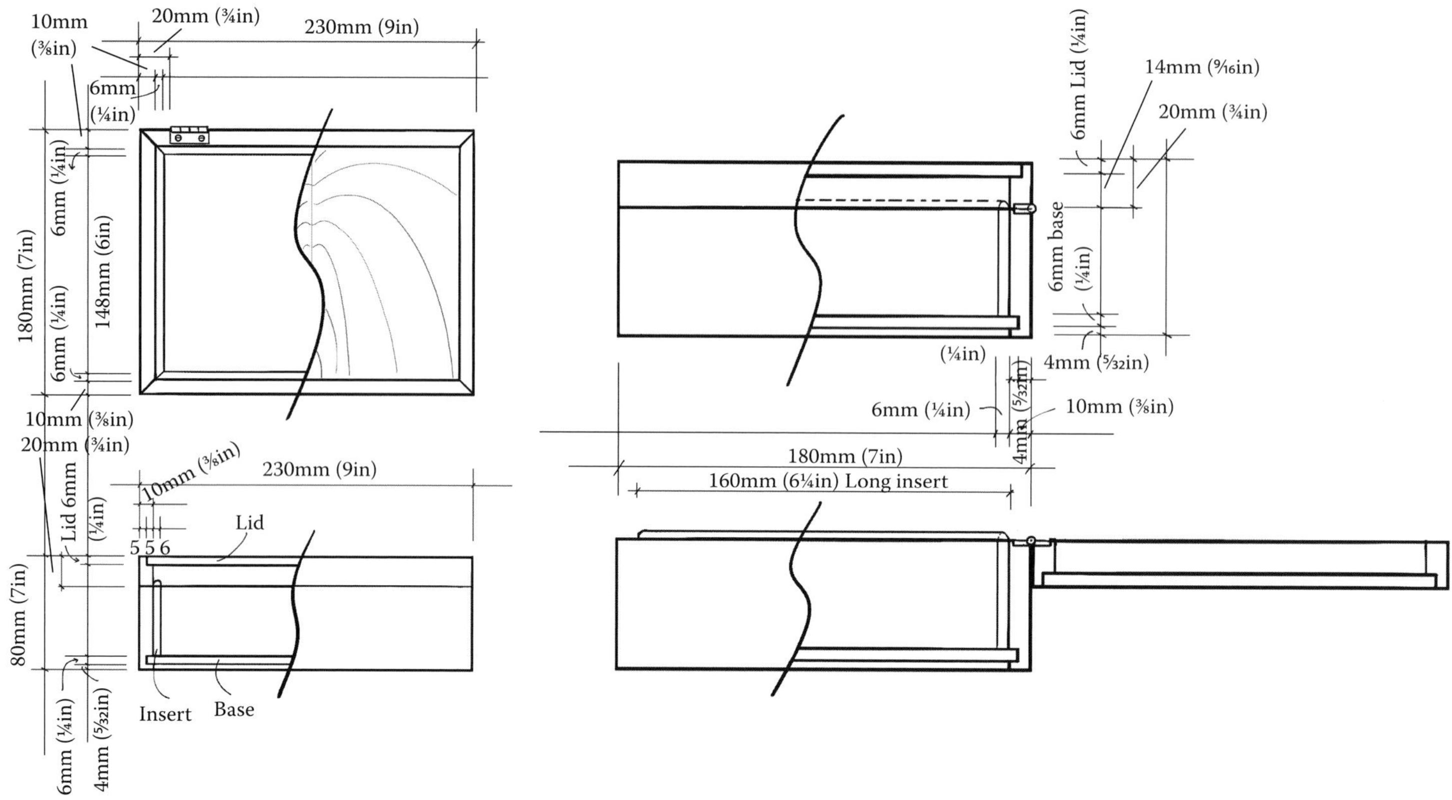

Illustration plan for a Mitred Keepsake Box.

Cutting List for a Mitred Keepsake Box

Part	No. of	Length	Width	Thickness	Material
Long sides	2	230mm (9in)	80mm (3⅛in)	10mm (⅜in)	Ash
Short sides	2	180mm (7in)	80mm (3⅛in)	10mm (⅜in)	Ash
Lid and base (include additional allowance for trim fitting)	2	220mm (8¾in)	170mm (6¾in)	6mm (¼in)	Veneered panel (Bird's eye maple and oak)
Long side inserts	2	210mm (8¼in)	55mm (2¼in)	6mm (¼in)	Teak
Short side inserts	2	160mm (6¼in)	55mm (2¼in)	6mm (¼in)	Teak

For this project I will be using mitres to join the sides, a slotted base and a fitted lid together. To hold the lid in place, inserts and/or the installation of hinges can be used. You will need four sides and two veneered panels. I am using ash wood for the sides, bookmatched birds-eye maple for the lid and oak for the bottom.

Whenever possible I will use one board of wood to make all four sides as the grain running along the faces will flow at least for three sides. This is especially so when I am using mitres to join the sides together. Otherwise, I would try to work off two boards to create one long side and one short side each and try to match the grain as much as possible.

BASIC BOX JOINERY

The following are common ways to attach the sides together. I have classified them into non-interlocking joints where most, if not all the strength comes from the adhesive used, and interlocking joints whereby there is some sort of mechanical attribute that makes them stronger. Move up so it follows on from previous line.

Non-interlocking joints:

1. Mitre joint
2. Rebate joint
3. Double rebate joint

Interlocking joints:

1. Finger joint
2. Dovetail joint
3. Mitred Dovetail joint

The following are common ways to attach the base to the box, which can also be used for attaching the lids.

1. Direct
2. Rebated or fitted
3. Slotted

These are just some common types of joinery used for box (and furniture) making. There are countless others each with their own strengths. Mix and match these joints to create your box projects.

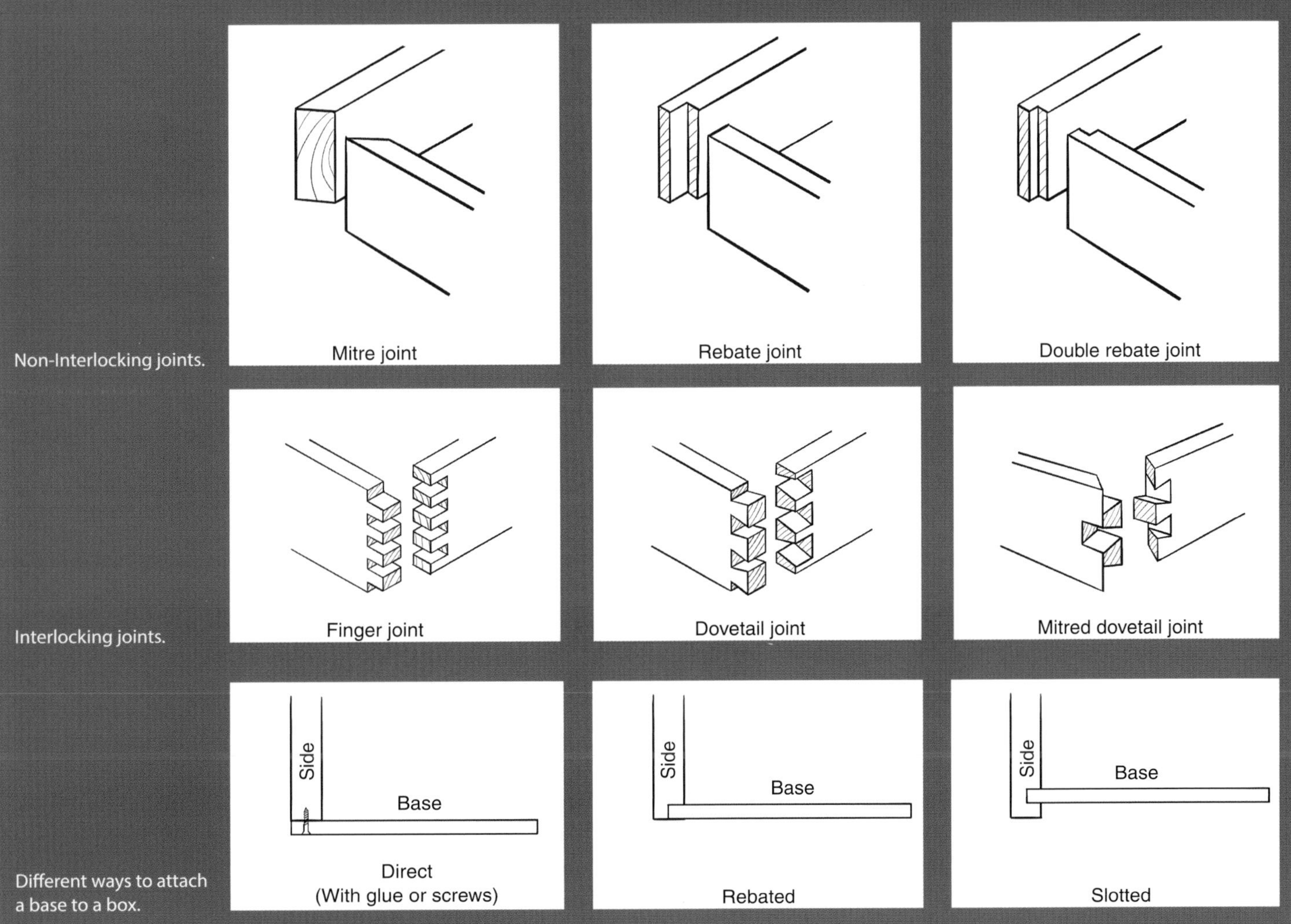

Non-Interlocking joints.

Interlocking joints.

Different ways to attach a base to a box.

MAKING A MITRED KEEPSAKE BOX

Prepare your pieces to size and cut your mitres. This can be done with a mitre jig over a shooting board, or by marking out and planing down by hand with a block plane.

Scribe out the rebates for the lid using a marking gauge. Using a plough or shoulder plane, create your rebates, making sure that the depth is able to accommodate the thickness of your veneered panel.

In this example, the grooves for the base are made using an electric router set up as a table router. This can also be done with a plough plane or with a chisel by first scribing out the position of the grooves.

Use tape to dry-fit the joints and fit the veneered base into the grooves, making sure that the base is slightly smaller to accommodate for any wood movement. All internal faces – the sides, lid and base – should be sanded and finished at this stage.

5

Apply PVA on the mitres and insert the base into the grooves. Ratchet straps are great for box making, especially when coupled with some rounded corner blocks to hold the workpiece in place during gluing-up. Check the box for squareness before tightening up the ratchet straps.

6

Slowly trim and fit the lid into the rebates of the box. During the fitting process, avoid forcing the lid into the rebate, as there will be no way to remove the lid if it is stuck. Once the lid is adjusted to size, apply PVA on the rebate and push the lid into place.

7

A pressing board that is slightly smaller than the lid is used together with clamps to apply even pressure all across. A practical tip is to use parcel tape on the surface and edges of the pressing board to prevent it from getting stuck to the box itself.

8

The edges of the box should be higher than the lid. Using a block plane, slowly remove the excess until the sides of the box are flush with the lid. Take note not to accidentally plane the veneered surface while doing so.

Using a marking gauge, scribe two lines to define the cut with ample space in between for the saw. The two lines will serve as guides for trimming down later. This approach ensures a precise and clean separation of the lid from the box.

Clamp the box onto your work surface and always keep two sides of the box in your line of sight to help you saw in a straight line. Slowly saw the lid apart. Once a side has been sawn through, rotate the box and continue sawing until the lid is separated from the base.

Once the lid has been separated from the base, you can follow the guide marks and trim the edges down. Secure your workpiece on the workbench and use a block plane to go around the edges. Be careful not to be over-zealous in this step, as you will end up chasing your own tail.

To ensure a perfect fit, you can prepare a set of mitred inserts that extend beyond the internal height of the base that act as the liner of the box. You may choose to have the liner at the base or the lid of the box.

Your box is now complete. You can end here if you are content with a box with a floating lid and can proceed with the finishing processes (*see* Chapter Nine). Otherwise, there are many other ways to further customise your box (*see* 'Elevating Your Box Projects' later in the chapter.).

FITTING HINGES

It can be terrifying to install hinges, as a badly positioned hinge will mean a wonky lid or a droopy door. I still make mistakes from time to time, and need 100 per cent concentration whenever I do any hinge installation. However, by understanding the basics of how a hinge works and what causes the usual problems, hinge installation may become a less stressful operation. I am using regular brass butt hinges. Be sure they are not twisted, warped or misaligned.

Common positions of the butt hinge in a box installation (view from the side):

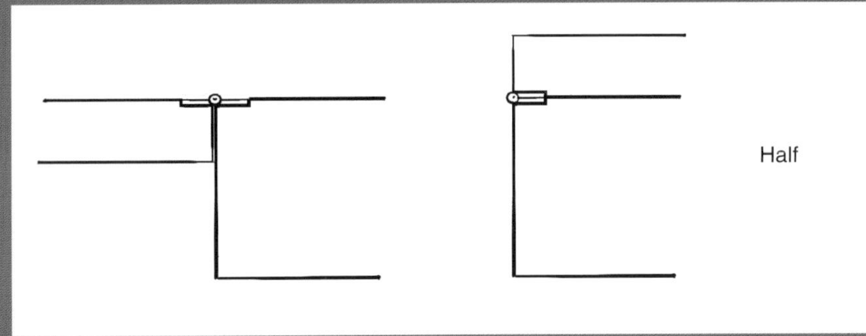

A half-moon hinge installation. The knuckle is set halfway into the side of the box and lid. The lid will open flat.

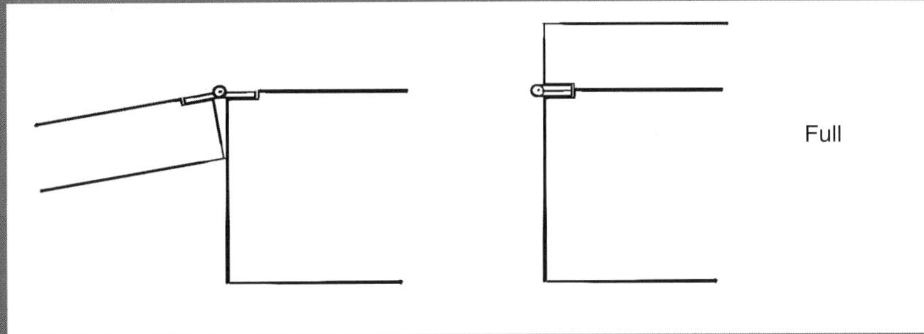

A full-moon hinge installation. The knuckle is set fully outside the box and lid. The lid will open past flat.

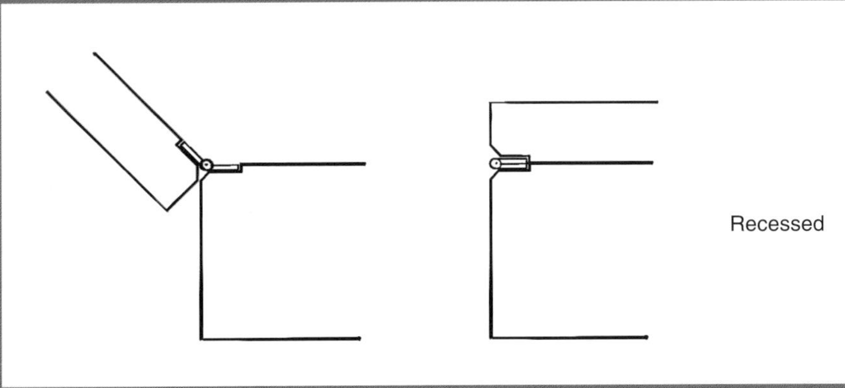

A shy-moon (recessed) hinge installation. The knuckle is fully recessed into the box and lid. The lid will not open flat.

INSTALLING HINGES

Place the hinges on the base of the box and use a knife to mark out their positions. Set a marking gauge to the thickness of the hinge leaf; this will be the depth that the hinge should sit into.

Scribe the depth with the marking gauge and remove the waste by sawing relief cuts then cleaning up with a chisel. Clamp a piece of wood behind to prevent any breakout when paring with the chisel.

Place the lid in an opened position, making sure it is squared with the base. Mark out the hinge locations and remove the waste. Place cards between the base and lid to allow a slight gap before marking out the hole positions for the screws.

Drill pilot holes and gently install the screws. Secure one screw on both parts at a time and check for any misalignment before driving in the remaining screws. Avoid removing and reinstalling screws repeatedly, as this can wear out the threads in the wood.

The box should close neatly and flush. However, there will be instances where the lid might not be aligned properly – this can be very common and is likely a wrongly positioned hinge. Take a step back and remove each screw one by one to see where the problem lies.

If all things fail and you are unable to rectify the issue, you could start afresh by drilling a hole and filling it up with a dowel. Sometimes a wooden skewer or chopstick could do the trick. Allow it to dry completely before proceeding again.

A properly installed hinge will close smoothly without any binding and with all sides flushed. To further enhance the look of your hinges, take some time to buff their surfaces with some metal polish and a soft cloth before the final installation.

The completed keepsake box, ideal for childhood treasures.

ELEVATING YOUR BOX PROJECTS

Here are some ideas to further enhance the visual and functional appeal of your box projects.

- ***Box base inserts*** Wrap some decorative fabric of your choice over cardboard or thin plywood and place it at the bottom of your box to add some colour to your boxes. You can increase its thickness and texture by using some felt or paper between the cloth and the cardboard. Sheets of foam can also be used to make thicker padded inserts for jewellery and watch boxes.
- ***Trays and dividers*** Use thin inserts as tray runners and make multiple trays with dividers. You can even design sloping runners for separate heights.
- ***Veneer keys and splines*** These not only add a decorative touch to the corners of a box, but also strengthen mitred boxes. Veneer keys are thin inserts placed into saw-cut grooves, while spines are thicker pieces that usually fit into grooves made with a router.
- ***Inlays and onlays*** These do not need to be large or elaborate. Simple small patterns can add elegance to an otherwise plain-looking surface. Once you have your pattern, trace it onto the surface, remove the top veneer in that area and replace it. Squares, rectangles and triangles are great shapes for beginners. For solid wood, use a router or router plane to remove a shallow layer of wood before fitting your pattern in place and flushing it flat later on.

SUMMARY

These projects are just some simple ideas that not only can beautify your home but more importantly give you confidence in creating wooden objects at home. By adapting these basic designs and techniques shown here and modifying them based on your needs, you can create your own wonderful and unique pieces.

Box base inserts can enhance the look of your boxes by adding colour and texture to the interior of your box.

Create compartments within your box by using trays and dividers.

Splines and veneer keys not only look pretty, they also strengthen mitre joints.

Experiment with basic geometric shapes, or try your hand at simple marquetry to add a unique touch to your box lids.

BIBLIOGRAPHY AND FURTHER READING

Crawford, Andrew *The Book of Boxes: The Complete Practical Guide to Design and Construction* (Guild of Master Craftsman Publications, 1993)

Forrester, Paul *Woodworker's Technique Bible* (Southwater, 2009)

Jones, Richard *Cut and Dried: A Woodworker's Guide to Timber Technology* (Lost Art Press, 2018)

Landis, Scott *The Workbench Book* (The Taunton Press Inc, 1987)

Odate, Toshio *Japanese Woodworking Tools* (The Taunton Press Inc, 1984)

Pourny, Christophe *The Furniture Bible* (Artisan, Workman Publishing Company, Inc, 2014)

Schleining, Lon *The Workbench* (The Taunton Press Inc, 2004)

Schwarz, Christopher *The Anarchist's Tool Chest* (Lost Art Press, 2011)

Schwarz, Christopher *The Anarchist's Workbench* (Lost Art Press, 2020)

Ulrich, Roger B. *Roman Woodworking* (Yale University Press, 2007)

Das Hausbucher der Mendelschen (The Nuremberg House Books, 1425–1806)

DK, *Woodwork: A Step-by-Step Photographic Guide to Successful Woodworking* (Dorling Kindersley, 2010)

Roman Workbench Instructional Video
https://lostartpress.com/collections/workbenches/products/video-build-a-roman-workbench

USEFUL LINKS AND RESOURCES

CITES (the Convention on International Trade in Endangered Species of Wild Fauna and Flora)
https://cites.org/eng
A guide to CITES- listed tree species.

The Wood Database
https://www.wood-database.com/
A large and ongoing information resource website on wood species around the world.

Lost Art Press
https://lostartpress.com/
An excellent selection of woodworking related books, tools, plans and online courses.

Wood Workers Workshop
http://woodworkersworkshop.co.uk/
An online tool shop run by woodworkers with a huge range of quality woodworking tools.

Workshop Heaven
https://workshopheaven.com/
An independent family-run business, providing tools to last a lifetime with long-term customer satisfaction.

Dieter Schmid Fine Tools
https://www.fine-tools.com/
A fine selection of outstanding woodworking tools and accessories.

Sjobergs
https://sjobergs.se/en
A Swedish maker of durable, well crafted workbenches and accessories for both hobbyist and professionals.

Mirka
https://www.mirka.com/en
Known for their wide range of abrasives, sanding and polishing tools, offering solutions for different surface finishing applications.

INDEX

First published in 2025 by
The Crowood Press Ltd
Ramsbury, Marlborough
Wiltshire SN8 2HR

enquiries@crowood.com
www.crowood.com

British Library Cataloguing-in-Publication Data
A catalogue record for this book is available from the British Library.

For product safety-related questions, contact:
productsafety@crowood.com

ISBN 978 0 7198 4567 3

Disclaimer
Safety is of the utmost importance in every aspect of woodworking. When using tools, always follow the manufacturer's safety guidelines and recommended procedures. Any use of the information found in this book is at the reader's own risk. The author and publisher assume no responsibility for any resulting accident, injury or damage.

Typeset by Envisage IT

Cover design by Samantha Rolfe-Hoang

Printed and bound in India by Thomson Press India

Dedication
To Dydy.
To my wife, Adelene – my greatest supporter, critic, and confidant. Without her, I might have never discovered woodworking.

Acknowledgments:
To all my teachers – both in woodworking and beyond, whose guidance nurtured my craft and, in turn, shaped the writing of this book.

To my friends, clients and students, whose trust and belief in my work have been invaluable throughout my journey – thank you.

Image on page 102 taken from 'Daedalus, Pasiphae and the wooden cow. Roman fresco from the northern wall of the triclinium in the Casa dei Vettii (VI 15,1) in Pompeii.' Image by Wolfgang Rieger, public domain, via Wikimedia Commons.